MICROS AT WORK

CASE STUDIES OF MICROCOMPUTERS IN LIBRARIES

Compiled by Jim Milliot
Introduction by Allan D. Pratt

Knowledge Industry Publications, Inc.
White Plains, NY and London

Professional Librarian Series

Micros at Work: Case Studies of Microcomputers in Libraries

Library of Congress Cataloging in Publication Data

Milliot, Jim.
    Micros at work.

    Bibliography: p.
    Includes index.
    1. Microcomputers—Library applications—Case studies.
2. Libraries—Automation—Case studies.   I. Title.
Z678.9.M478   1985   025.3′028′54   85-241
ISBN 0-86729-117-6
ISBN 0-86729-116-8 (pbk.)

Printed in the United States of America

10 9 8 7 6 5 4 3 2 1

Table of Contents

List of Tables and Figures

Part I

Introduction

by Allan D. Pratt

There has been much talk of the "micro revolution," but "revolution" is not quite apt. It might better be called the "micro reformation." Computers per se are nothing very new or dramatic in libraries. Large, or at least moderately large, computers are now an integral part of the operations of many libraries. The antipathy toward "soulless machines" which was evident 20 years ago among some librarians has now fairly well abated. The use of computers for circulation control, cataloging and many other purposes is now so routine as to be unremarkable—no more novel or innovative than the telephone.

However, until recently, librarians, along with many others whose daily work has brought them in contact with computers, really have not had much say in the design, selection or application of computer systems. The real decisions about how the computer system should be designed and used, and what it should do, have been made by the programmers, systems analysts, project directors and, of course, directors of data processing. Those who have worked with large-scale computer centers, whether in a library or elsewhere, are all too familiar with the intricacies of getting a project implemented. There are elaborate procedures for justifying a project. Endless meetings are required to explicate what is wanted, and simple projects seem to take forever.

This problem, familiar as it is to all who have worked with large, centralized computer centers, is even more difficult for librarians. While

1

the computer center staff usually has some familiarity with the problems in other departments, their lack of knowledge regarding library requirements has been encyclopedic. This has frequently led to misunderstandings, confusion and unsuccessful attempts at automation. It has also led both parties to conclude that the other is hopelessly ignorant.

After many years of accepting direction from centralized staffs or centers, a growing number of librarians began to propose that librarians become more involved with computer services, in order to better serve their needs. This was an attractive idea to librarians, but not to data processing departments. Those who have been involved in an attempt to get approval for a computer system independent of the local DP department can bear witness to the intensity of the battles often fought in such meetings.

By and large, however, librarians continued to persevere and library automation gained widespread popularity after systems specifically designed for libraries came into being. After CLSI, Data Phase and others began selling turnkey systems, library computerization became fairly common. While turnkey systems only permit a certain amount of flexibility, and none are *exactly* suited to a particular library, their use in libraries has allowed librarians to refer to "main entry" with some assurance that vendors will not think they are talking about the library's front door.

The increasing capabilities of these dedicated systems have enabled libraries to run their own systems, independent of the larger institutional data processing centers. The newer turnkey systems are more library-oriented than earlier systems, but they still require that the library staff do things in a particular way. Although they do allow some tailoring to meet local needs, by and large they can perform only those tasks for which they were specifically programmed. Effecting changes is still almost as difficult as before.

Microcomputers embody the "every man his own preacher" vision. They offer the hope that one can find relief from some of one's administrative burdens without the intercession of others. Not only are these inexpensive systems under the direct control of the librarian, they are also completely open-ended in terms of programming. Within an extremely wide range of possibilities, a micro can do *anything* you want it to.

Even a modest degree of control over one's own fate can be extraordinarily powerful. Peters and Waterman, in *In Search of Excellence*, describe an experiment that shows how powerful this sense of control can be. Two groups of people were given complex puzzles and proofreading tasks to perform. There was a great deal of noise in the background—people talking, machines running, etc. One group was simply directed to perform the tasks. The second group was provided with a button to push which would turn off the noise. The group with the off switch solved five times the number of puzzles and made only a fraction of the errors in proofreading as compared to the other group. "Now for the kicker. . . 'none of the subjects in the off switch group ever used the switch. The mere knowledge that one can exert control made the difference.' "[1]

Given the opportunity to experiment with computer power in the form of micros, librarians have responded rapidly. The micro has released a reservoir of previously untapped creativity. This volume is itself evidence of how the situation has changed. Librarians are using micros, and are pushing the capabilities to the limit. Most libraries described here are routinely using word processing and spreadsheet programs. Some are using database management programs and some are doing original programming. Schuyler at Kitsap Regional Library, Wismer at the Maine State Library and Jolly at the Glendora (CA) Public Library are just a few of the many in the country who have accepted the challenge of the micro, bending it to their objectives so that they can better perform their duties.

Though you may not often choose to write your own programs, you can if you wish. The button is there, even if you don't push it. This freedom—freedom from bureaucratic overhead and administrative regulation, from vendor's decisions about how things are to be done, freedom to do it your way—is exhilarating. You can regain some control over your library, control that over the years may have been surrendered to centralization, to consortia, to networks and to the multitude of other organizations which have somehow constrained your operations. True, it may be a lot of work to do it yourself, especially in the early stages of a micro project. Sometimes "do it yourself" isn't worth it, but the knowledge that you can do it is worth something in its own right.

---

1. Thomas J. Peters and Robert H. Waterman Jr., *In Search of Excellence* (New York: Harper & Row, 1982).

You, as librarian in a small library, or in a small branch of a big system, no longer need to accept everything as decreed from others. You can buy, or write, a program that analyzes your budget in ways that are appropriate for your specific branch or library—despite the fact that the main library may do it differently. You can write a program to do something useful and get it done. These programs are usually not monumentally complex. Often they represent the little change or the slight improvement which converts a useless *pro forma* report into a truly helpful one.

Until recently, librarians would accept systems or procedures which didn't seem quite right, either because they didn't know that things could be done differently or because the systems had been designed by experts. But now they will be able to look at the designer or salesperson and say "With my Apple II and a $200 program I can do X, Y and Z. And you tell me that your elaborate and expensive system can do only X? Come now, you can do better than that."

While this scenario is obviously somewhat exaggerated, it is not an exaggeration to predict that micros will cause many changes in libraries, and that most of these changes will be for the better. However, the changes will not occur without some effort. The introduction of a new way of doing things means that a lot of learning has to go on.

Not only do people need to learn about micros, they need to learn *how* to learn about them. All is not necessarily smooth sailing with micros in every library. A little reading between the lines of some of the profiles contained in this volume suggests that micros were not an unmixed blessing in every instance. Matters can go awry for any number of reasons—physical, environmental or psychological. Observation, and common sense, suggest that imposition of micros by edict will be less successful than a gradual introduction such as Wismer used. He put the micro on a wheeled cart so that it could be moved from department to department. The staff was largely self-taught. Within a year of introduction, the departments demanded their own micros.

The first question that comes to the mind of the novice is, "What can you use a micro for?" To which a reasonable answer might be, "What can you use a pencil and a pad of paper for?" You can balance your checkbook, calculate next year's budget, write the great American novel, make a grocery list, draw portraits, compose music or doodle—the list is endless. Just so with a micro. It, like the pencil and paper, is a tool of great flexibilty and versatility.

There are indeed many things to do with pencil and paper; however in most organizations, including libraries, there are only two things that actually get done. You either push words around or you push numbers around. Once you've accomplished either of these tasks, you have two choices: you can send that piece of paper to somebody else, or save it in your files (or most likely both). By no strange coincidence, a great proportion of the currently available programs for micros do one or more of these same tasks. Word processing programs push words around; spreadsheet and other accounting programs push numbers around; telecommunications programs send your work to others at the speed of light; database management systems save your work, filing it for future reference and modification.

These "big four" procedures—words and numbers to be manipulated in some fashion, then to be sent or saved—are common in virtually every facet of our contemporary "information society," in libraries as well as corporations, government bodies and a multitude of other organizations. In most instances, a program that performs one of these tasks well for a business will perform equally well for a library.

In libraries, word processing is far and away the most common use of micros. Surveys have shown that word processing is cited more frequently than all other applications combined. This is quite understandable, since libraries have so much repetitive typing to do, the very task that word processing handles so well. The oddity is that it took so long for librarians to become aware of this. Word processing systems have been around for perhaps 15 years as "dedicated systems" from Wang, IBM and other companies, but they still are relatively rare in libraries. While it is now generally conceded that dedicated WP systems are being displaced by micros, it is odd that when they were so popular, libraries largely ignored them.

Unlike word processing, the electronic spreadsheet programs, exemplified by VisiCalc, have no prior history of earlier versions and implementations. (Not that somebody couldn't have developed a spreadsheet program for earlier minicomputers; it's just that nobody did.)

Though they are newer, spreadsheet programs share one important characteristic with word processing. Neither is smart. Word processing programs are basically just clever typewriters. Once you learn the magic keystrokes to make the program work, you have it. The hard part isn't learning the program's details. The hard part is the writing—figuring out what you're going to write before you actually write it down and let the program make it look neat. Spreadsheet programs require the same kind of thinking in advance. The hard part isn't learning how to put a formula in this cell or a caption in that one; it's knowing what to put where. This is the grimmer aspect of the freedom offered by micros. If you are going to do it yourself rather than accept someone else's definition of what "it" is, you have to *think* about what you're trying to accomplish. With freedom comes responsibility.

Using a micro for the sending and receiving of either words or numbers over the telephone line is conceptually pretty straightforward. While there are many technicalities that can corrupt the process, it is not very difficult to understand what is going on. This is not to denigrate the value of telecommunications programs nor the skills of their authors. In fact, present communications programs are so well done that their use is virtually transparent: learning how to use such a program is slightly more difficult than learning how to make a long-distance telephone call. Once learned, the program can be used in less time than it takes to make that call.

Database management programs (DBMS) on the other hand are an entirely different matter. They are not simple and transparent. They are frequently complex. However, librarians need take a back seat to no one when it comes to databases and methods for managing them. They've been maintaining very complex ones for years—the card catalog, serials control, name and subject authority files and so on. And no one would deny that AACR 2, ALA filing rules and MARC formats get high marks for complexity.

Librarians seem to have difficulty working with the computer-based DBMS for a curious reason. They already know too much. It's easier to convert a nonbeliever to your religion than it is to convert one of another faith. The nonbeliever doesn't have as much to unlearn and, never having experienced any other set of rules, doesn't ask as many questions about why things are the way they are.

Thus, those who are totally unfamiliar with micro database management systems can adapt to them with relatively little trauma. However, a librarian looking at a DMBS is initially confused by the use of new names for familiar concepts and later appalled at the system's limited capabilities. The widely known micro DBMS programs are adequate for more or less standard kinds of problems, such as inventory control, personnel records and the like. Their performance with bibliographic records is marginal at best. Indeed, it is possible to develop library systems with these DBMS', as the profiles describing the Glendora (CA) Public Library and the Ekstrom Library at the University of Louisville attest. However, these systems are not dealing with full and complex MARC-style records.

"Off the shelf" programs meet only some of the library's needs. Just as the civil engineer needs stress analysis programs which would be useless to the chemist, so the librarian needs serials control and cataloging programs useless to any other profession. The need for these special programs is gradually being met. As librarians and programmers become better acquainted with the capabilities of micros, and as a deeper understanding of the practical problems and sensible solutions develops, we will see more of them. Victor Rosenberg's programs which prepare bibliographies, Robert Kepple's cataloging and acquisitions programs, "Checkmate" for serials control from CLASS, Betty Costa's COMPUTER CAT, and many others, are now available.

Some programs now available are relatively primitive. They work, though not always as well as one might wish. But new insights and new designs will be forthcoming. Currently, most of the programs emulate what we were doing before, just as the first automobiles were horseless carriages. We will soon see programs that go beyond this emulation stage, though it is quite pointless to speculate on just what form this progress may take.

Even with commercially available programs for the routine word and number shuffling and with special purpose library programs for unique tasks, a gap still remains. Sometimes there is simply nothing available to do what you want to do. Sometimes the programs that are available just don't quite do it the way you need it; you have to do it yourself. And sometimes you can persuade yourself that it really *is* necessary to do it yourself, even if it isn't. This can occur because developing a program, a spreadsheet or just a clever way of doing something can be a lot of fun. There is a very real sense of enjoyment and accomplishment when you, for example, develop a spreadsheet that allows you to do in a few minutes something that previously took an hour.

Tracing the growth of micros in libraries, we can see that librarians have played a changing role. The first micros appeared in libraries, or more likely in learning resource centers, as objects to be "managed" for patrons. They were treated like movie projectors, videotape players or phonographs—as "hardware" necessary to use some particular medium—16mm film, videotape, records, computer programs. At first, this seemed reasonable. Another medium, another device to "play" it. Just like all the other fads over the last 50 years. But it wasn't the same. There's only so much to be learned about how a projector or videotape player works. But learning where the power switch is, and which way to put the floppy disk in the drive, isn't enough for micros. It's only the beginning.

Librarians, especially school librarians, were besieged by questioners—teachers and students alike. Considering the fact that no one—in or out of the computer business—expected micros to catch on the way they did, it is not surprising that librarians were unprepared for this onslaught. Considering the habits of librarians, it is also not surprising that there was an explosion of workshops, meetings and seminars on micros all over the country. Librarians made it a point to find out about these funny new machines. It was almost a point of professional pride. They learned about them, at least initially, so that they could answer their patrons' questions. It was not until later that librarians began to give serious thought to using micros for their own purposes.

Patron access to micros is unique to libraries. Most other institutions would be horrified at the thought of complete strangers wandering in and "bashing away" at their micros. But this is routine in many libraries. Dewey describes his experiences at the North Pulaski Branch of the Chicago Public Library; Smith describes her experiences at the Lorain (OH) Public Library. As is often the case with new innovations, people try different ways of achieving the same end.

Despite the *possibility* of "every man his own preacher," it is unlikely that micro applications will flourish in libraries along completely divergent paths. There are two reasons for this. In the first place, a fairly high degree of standardization does, in a sense, hold the profession together. Such things as AACR 2 and the MARC formats are recognized communications channels. One invents a new cataloging format at the risk of being totally isolated from the mainstream of professional activity. These standards are important. In fact, they are too little followed. We already have more idiosyncratic variations than we should.

Apart from the noncomformists, librarians have had a longstanding tradition of working together. Interlibrary loans, cooperative arrangements, consortia and other forms of joint endeavor for mutual benefit predate micros by at least a century. Interestingly, a strong spirit of cooperation has developed among microcomputer users as well. It dates from the mid 1970s, the era of the "computer hacker" who most probably soldered a micro together from a kit. These early users formed groups and clubs through which they could share their knowledge and their programs. These efforts have grown into what is now an elaborate network, whose members keep in touch via both conventional and electronic mail. All these groups have extensive collections of programs which are in the public domain, and which are exchanged for only the cost of copying.

We are now seeing the confluence of both these lines of cooperation. Virginia Eager of GTE Laboratories has recently published a directory of microcomputer user groups which focuses on library applications. Her second edition lists 32 such groups in the United States, five in Canada and one in Belgium. In addition, at least two national centers for the exchange of public domain software are currently operating. Eric Anderson, of Freeport (IL) is running an exchange center for Apple software. His collection contains VisiCalc templates and DB Master files for such things as library budgeting and AV equipment inventories. For the IBM Personal Computer there is the new OCLC Microcomputer Program Exchange (OMPX). Its collection includes several utility programs to simplify the system's use, as well as library-specific programs. In the latter category, for example, is a program called CLEANER, which "cleans up" files downloaded from BRS by removing the search statements, typos, billing information, etc.

Now that librarians have become familiar with micros as "stand-alone" devices they are becoming increasingly interested in micros as communications devices. Though micros were not originally designed as such, they can replace the old "dumb terminals" for online database searching. With the addition of a modem and a telecommunications program, the micro becomes a "supersmart terminal" capable of transmitting previously recorded search queries and retaining on disk the results of searches. This latter ability, downloading, is an excellent example of the kind of local control that micros allow. With a dumb terminal, the only thing you can do with retrieved citations is print them on whatever kind of paper your terminal uses. If you want to incorporate the citations into another document, or do anything else with them, you have to retype them.

With a micro, you can save those citations on a disk, edit them, incorporate citations from other sources, include them as part of a longer document, and so forth. Using a micro for searching not only improves the quality of the search process, it also improves the quality of the final product.

The use of a micro in lieu of a terminal has become so popular with librarians that several of the major database vendors have adapted their systems to allow easier searching with micros. Furthermore, the major bibliographic utilities (RLIN, OCLC and WLN) have now reached the same conclusion that individual librarians reached earlier— that micros are preferable to terminals. All three have chosen a microcomputer to replace what were at best "semismart" terminals.

This agreement that micros are preferable to special purpose terminals seems to be based simply on technological imperatives rather than on a formal meeting of minds. There were such compelling reasons to switch to micros that all the groups reached the same conclusion independently. And indeed they were right. A few years ago, librarians were expressing concern that their desks would be cluttered with multiple terminals; one for Dialog, one for OCLC, one for the New York Times, one for LEXIS and so on. Fortunately, this problem has now faded away. Today any vendor who required a dedicated special purpose terminal to access his data files would find it very difficult to sell to librarians. Ten years ago it might have been necessary; today librarians know better.

The major bibliographic utilities' decision to go with micros is perhaps more far-reaching than was first realized. Micros will now be installed in many libraries that otherwise might never have considered them. And the micros, just by virtue of being there, will be available to librarians who otherwise wouldn't have had access to them. These librarians will begin to find uses for these micros that the utilities probably hadn't thought of. Perhaps these same librarians, who doubted they'd ever see a micro in their jobs, will be the authors of the next volume like this one.

The following chapters relate the adventures of some of the early converts to micros. You will find nothing in them which reflects the despair you feel when you realize you just forgot to save that file you had worked on for three hours; nothing about the fatigue of a 2:00 a.m debugging session; nothing about your satisfaction (*joy* is not too strong a word) when your program finally runs. But hidden beneath these rather bland descriptions are many such adventures, defeats and victories. Read them; learn from them. Then go and do likewise.

Part II

Results of the Microcomputer Survey

This book is based on a survey of microcomputer use in libraries conducted by Knowledge Industry Publications, Inc. during the spring and fall of 1984. Questionnaires were sent to 220 libraries in the United States and Canada, and 64 usable responses were received. Of these, 28 came from academic libraries (universities, high schools and grammar schools), 25 from public libraries and 11 from special libraries (government, corporate and medical).

MICROCOMPUTER OWNERSHIP

The study indicates that three microcomputers have dominated the library marketplace in the early 1980s: Apple, Radio Shack and IBM. Of these, Apple has been the most popular choice. Of the 64 libraries that responded to the survey, 54, or 84%, reported that they owned an Apple micro. Within the Apple family the Apple II+ had the most support, with 28 libraries (44%) owning that particular Apple model. (See Table 1.)

The Apple is a particular favorite at academic libraries where 96% of the librarians responding to the survey reported owning an Apple. The widespread use of Apples at academic libraries is attributable in

Table 1: Microcomputer Ownership, by Type of Library

Company	Percent Owned All	Percent Owned Academic	Percent Owned Public	Percent Owned Special
Apple line	84%	96%	84%	55%
II+	44	43	52	27
IIe	27	36	20	18
II	11	11	12	9
Lisa	2	3	0	0
Macintosh	2	3	0	0
TRS-80 line	38	29	48	36
Model II	19	14	20	27
Model III	11	7	20	0
Model 12	3	0	3	9
Model 16	2	0	4	0
Model IV	2	0	4	0
Model 100	2	3	0	0
IBM Line	31	39	24	27
PC	14	14	12	18
PC/XT	14	21	12	0
OCLC (modified)	3	3	0	9

large measure to the large number of Apples in place in the nation's classrooms. According to a survey conducted by Market Data Retrieval, a compiler of high school and grammar school mailing lists, Apples were found in approximately 67% of all public schools that owned micros for a nearly 50% market share.[1] Because of Apple's dominant position in the school market, academic librarians interested in eventually creating a networking system within their school often chose the Apple to ensure that the library's machines could be integrated with other micros. Furthermore, school libraries that make their micros available for student use choose Apple since it is the micro with which more students are familiar.

The use of Apples at public libraries, while not as pervasive as at

---

[1] Data from Market Data Retrieval as reported in the *Educational Marketer*, September 16, 1983.

academic libraries, is nonetheless extensive. Some 84% of the public libraries reported owning an Apple. The reasons cited most often by librarians for choosing Apples include low maintenance cost and operating reliability, ease of use, uncomplicated instructions, moderate price, software availability and, in some cases, its compatibility with other school micros. In addition, because of the availability of software, Apples are the preferred choice of libraries which make their machines available to the public.

Although claiming only 55% of the special library respondents, Apples are still the most widely owned micros in government, medical and corporate libraries. At special libraries, Apples are generally owned in combination with other micros. Micros that are less popular, such as the NCR Worksaver, tend to be the only micro where they are in place, since they are less likely to be compatible with other micros.

Radio Shack's TRS-80 models are the second most popular micros in libraries. The TRS-80 is most popular at public libraries where 48% of the respondents said they own a Radio Shack brand. Radio Shack's second place ranking notwithstanding, the TRS-80s are only used by 38% of the libraries in the survey, a considerable drop from the 84% mark enjoyed by Apple. Librarians selecting TRS-80s were usually influenced by price considerations and ease of use. Most librarians familiar with the TRS-80 machines praised their reliability. However, some complained that maintenance was slow when the micros required anything more than minor repairs—often the hardware had to be sent out of house and it would not be returned for a month.

The IBM line, in use by 31% of the libraries in the survey, is most popular at academic institutions. Some 39% of the academic libraries reported that they own an IBM compared to 27% of the special libraries and 24% of public libraries. IBM's popularity at academic libraries stems in part from university familiarity with IBM mainframe computers. Several colleges reported they chose the IBM micro with an eye toward eventually creating a network system to the college mainframe.

Although the IBM line is only the third most popular micro at libraries, there are indications its popularity is increasing. IBM entered the micro field after both Apple and Radio Shack, but has been increasing its share of the micro market in all areas, including libraries. Libraries that have only recently started acquiring micro capabilities (since spring 1984) seem to be buying IBMs in almost equal amounts with the Apple. Librarians are attracted to the IBM because of its reputation; they believe that the company can be counted on to back its products. Of equal significance to librarians is their belief that the greatest amount of new software will be written for the IBM.

Librarians were very positive in their evaluations of all three brands of microcomputers. Almost without exception librarians reported that the hardware operated with no serious breakdowns. Reliability of operation led many librarians to forego buying service contracts in the belief that the average 10% of purchase price charge was not justified by the maintenance requirements. There has, however, been some flip-flopping on the service contract issue. Some libraries that have not had service contracts in the past said they would consider adding a contract if their micro operation increased to any great degree. On the other hand, some libraries that have had contracts reported that they won't renew them because the contracts did not prove cost-effective. The library most likely to have a service contract is one that has a relatively large number of micros but one that is not large enough to have its own maintenance staff.

APPLICATIONS

The exploration of different applications of micros in libraries is hampered by the fact that micro programs in most libraries are run in a highly informal, decentralized manner. Micros have generally been introduced by one or two computer advocates who then find themselves overseeing the micro program with little formal guidelines or established procedures. Because supervising the micro operation is often an extra duty of one or two staff members, librarians are often forced to scramble to find time to establish micro applications.

Being pressed for time in implementing micro applications, librarians tend to begin with a function that is the simplest to establish and one that can be used by a wide number of people—word processing. The overwhelming consensus among librarians was that word processing applications alone justified acquiring micros. Using micros for routine, everyday tasks such as writing letters and memos allows staff members to complete these tasks more quickly and more accurately.

The survey indicates that 86% of all libraries use micros for general management applications such as word processing and budget analysis. Catalog, list and bibliography generation, which also involve some word processing work, ranked second (61%). Database development is being used by 38% of the libraries, and is the category that appeared to be the fastest growing. As librarians gain experience with micros, most are eager to use the technology to create small databases that previously were not cost-effective to do by hand (such as cataloging a collection of fewer than 100 items).

Although general management was the top application at all three types of libraries surveyed, there are some significant shifts among the different libraries for various other applications. For example, 3% of academic libraries use micros for acquisitions while 32% of public libraries find micros helpful for this application. Similarly, computer-assisted instruction was used in 40% of public libraries, but only 18% of special libraries. (See Table 2.)

A majority of libraries (55%) have micros that are made available for patron use. Publicly available micros are in place at 76% of the public libraries, 46% of the academic libraries and 27% of the special libraries. At public libraries programs for patron use of micros vary widely from library to library. Some libraries have established a com-

Table 2: Applications of Microcomputers, by Type of Library

Application	Percent In Use All	Percent In Use Academic	Percent In Use Public	Percent In Use Special
General management	86%	89%	84%	82%
Catalogs, lists, bibliographies	61	64	56	64
Local database development	47	39	44	73
Remote database searching	38	43	16	73
Computer-assisted instruction	31	29	40	18
Local database searching	25	29	16	36
Circulation control/backup	20	18	20	27
Acquisitions	17	3	32	18
Interlibrary loan	17	14	20	18
Serials control	14	7	16	27
A/V control	14	14	16	9
Online catalog	11	14	4	18
Reserve book room	3	7	0	0

prehensive public access micro program, complete with orientation classes, booking procedures and computer literacy classes. Other libraries take the opposite track, providing little more than access to the machines and software. Although some libraries charge a small fee for using the micros, most libraries make them available free of charge. Most libraries view public access micros as a way to attract new patrons to the library, and as a good public relations tool, rather than as a means of generating additional funds. Special libraries also tend to see micros as increasing the prestige of the library within their institutions.

SOFTWARE

Easy-to-learn programs are important to librarians, since most in-house training is minimal. Extensive, formal training for librarians on using micros is more the exception than the rule. Most libraries conduct brief training sessions on the fundamentals of operating the machines, and then staff members are expected to pick it up as they go along. Despite the less than overwhelming training offered to librarians, most survey respondents said staff resistance to using the micros was minimal. The surest way to overcome any resistance is to show reluctant staff members how using micros can make their jobs easier.

The sophistication of libraries' various micro operations is a mixed bag. Reflecting this mixture is the nearly equal division between libraries that develop their own software (48%) and libraries that do not produce software in-house (52%). The greater a library's commitment to micros, especially at public and academic institutions, the more likely that library is to have a staff member who is interested, and able, to develop some in-house programs. At special libraries, which reported the least amount of in-house software development (36%), the biggest roadblock to software production tends to be restrictions imposed by staff size. Indeed all librarians complained that heavy workloads hindered their ability to explore methods for using micros most effectively. (See Table 3.)

The most popular software packages owned by libraries parallel the most frequently used applications. VisiCalc is the only software package owned by a majority of libraries; 55% of the libraries reported that they own this spreadsheet program. WordStar (22%), Apple Writer

Table 3: Microcomputer Use in Libraries

Survey Question		All Libraries	Academic	Public	Special
Is your micro part of an integrated system?	no	(54)[1] 84%	(23) 82%	(22) 88%	(9) 82%
	yes	(10) 16	(5) 18	(3) 12	(2) 18
Is your micro available for patron use?	no	(29) 45	(15) 54	(6) 24	(8) 73
	yes	(35) 55	(13) 46	(19) 76	(3) 27
Has your library developed its own software?	no	(33) 52	(14) 50	(12) 48	(7) 64
	yes	(31) 48	(14) 50	(13) 52	(4) 36
Does your library expect to purchase additional software?	no	(5) 8	(2) 7	(2) 8	(1) 9
	yes	(53) 83	(22) 79	(22) 88	(9) 82
	unsure	(6) 9	(4) 14	(1) 4	(1) 9
Does your library expect to develop its own software?	no	(35) 55	(14) 50	(15) 60	(6) 55
	yes	(21) 33	(9) 32	(8) 32	(4) 36
	unsure	(8) 13	(5) 18	(2) 8	(1) 9

[1]The figures in parentheses indicate the number of respondents; the figures that follow represent that number as a percentage of all responses.

(16%), Scripsit (11%) and Bank Street Writer (9%) are other popular software programs and all are used in word processing. dBase II, the second most popular software package at 26%, is a database program and is indicative of librarians' growing interest in this application. (See Table 4.)

Librarians were generally pleased with the quality of software available, although there was agreement that more library-specific software should be developed. The most frequently voiced complaint was that WordStar is too complicated for beginning micro users to understand.

THE STATISTICS

The tables that follow are summaries of the 64 usable responses that Knowledge Industry Publications, Inc. received from academic, public and special libraries. These tables are designed to serve as a cross

Table 4: Commercial Software Packages Owned by Libraries

Software	Number of Libraries	
VisiCalc	(35)[1]	55%
dBase II	(17)	26
WordStar	(14)	22
Apple Writer	(10)	16
PFS: Report	(10)	16
PFS: File	(9)	14
VisiFile	(8)	13
DB Master	(7)	11
Lotus 1-2-3	(7)	11
Scripsit	(7)	11
Bank Street Writer	(6)	9
Profile	(6)	9
Multiplan	(4)	6
CrossTalk	(4)	6
Screen Writer	(4)	6
SuperCalc	(4)	6
Volkswriter	(4)	6
PFS: Graph	(3)	5
Superscripsit	(3)	5
Data Factory	(3)	5
Profile III+	(3)	5
VisiPlot	(3)	5
VisiTrend	(3)	5
VisiDex	(2)	3
Multimate	(2)	3
Superterm	(2)	3
Overdue Writer	(2)	3
Scripsit II	(2)	3
Typing Tutor	(2)	3

[1]The figures in parentheses indicate the number of respondents; the figures that follow represent that number as a percentage of all responses.

reference to the statistics presented earlier in this introduction. The first section gives summary tables for all libraries. It is followed by summary tables for academic, public and special libraries.

The balance of this book is devoted to profiles of libraries that responded to the questionnaire. The survey information has been supplemented with follow-up phone calls. In most cases, the libraries that are described in the profiles were chosen because they have been successful in implementing at least one application at their institution, and have had some time to evaluate the effectiveness of their microcomputer programs.

Each profile describes when, why and how a library chose to enter the age of the microcomputer. Some micro applications presented are unique to a particular library, such as the database system developed at the Fry Collection of the Yale Medical Library for its collection of medical paintings and drawings. More often, the applications presented are of general interest: i.e., how different libraries use micros for standard library functions such as acquisitions, cataloging, interlibrary loan and reserve lists as well as for administrative purposes such as mailing lists, accounting and correspondence.

Several appendixes have been provided at the end of this book to give readers further information. The questionnaire which formed the basis for this survey is reproduced in Appendix A. Appendix B lists the address, telephone number and contact for each of the libraries profiled. In Appendix C readers will find the names and addresses of selected microcomputer hardware and software vendors. A glossary of terms and a selected bibliography are supplied at the end of this book.

Table 5: Statistical Summary of Survey Responses

ALL LIBRARIES

Microcomputer Use
(64 Responses)

Is your micro part of an integrated system?	no	(54)[1]	84%
	yes	(10)	16
Is your micro available for patron use?	no	(29)	45
	yes	(35)	55
Has your library developed its own software?	no	(33)	52
	yes	(31)	48
Does your library expect to purchase additional software?	no	(5)	8
	yes	(53)	83
	unsure	(6)	9

[1]The figures in parentheses indicate the number of respondents; the figures that follow represent that number as a percentage of all responses.

Table 5: Statistical Summary of Survey Responses (continued)

Does your library expect to develop its own software?		no	(35)	55%
		yes	(21)	33
		unsure	(8)	13

Applications

General management	(55)	86%
Catalogs, lists, bibliographies	(39)	61
Local database development	(30)	47
Remote database searching	(24)	38
Computer-assisted instruction	(20)	31
Local database searching	(16)	25
Circulation control/backup	(13)	20
Acquisitions	(11)	17
Interlibrary loan	(11)	17
Serials control	(9)	14
A/V control	(9)	14
Online catalog	(7)	11
Reserve book room	(2)	3

Microcomputer Ownership

Apple line (total)	(54)	84%
II+	(28)	44
IIe	(17)	27
II	(7)	11
Lisa	(1)	2
Macintosh	(1)	2
Atari 800	(3)	5
Commodore line (total)	(6)	9%
Vic	(4)	6
Pet	(1)	2
64	(1)	2
Compaq	(2)	3
Franklin	(2)	3
Hewlett-Packard 125	(2)	3%
IBM line (total)	(20)	31%
PC	(9)	14
PC/XT	(9)	14
OCLC (modified)	(2)	3

Table 5: Statistical Summary of Survey Responses (continued)

North Star Horizon	(2)	3%
Osborne	(2)	3%
TRS-80 line (total)	(24)	38%
Model II	(12)	19
Model III	(7)	11
Model 12	(2)	3
Model 16	(1)	2
Model IV	(1)	2
Model 100	(1)	2
Vector Graphics	(2)	3%

ACADEMIC LIBRARIES
(University, High School, Grammar School)

Microcomputer Use
(28 Responses)

Is your library part of an integrated system?	no	(23)[1]	82%
	yes	(5)	18
Is your micro available for patron use?	no	(15)	54
	yes	(13)	46
Has your library developed its own software?	no	(14)	50
	yes	(14)	50
Does your library expect to purchase additional software?	no	(2)	7
	yes	(22)	79
	unsure	(4)	14
Does your library expect to develop its own software?	no	(14)	50
	yes	(9)	32
	unsure	(5)	18

Applications
General management	(25)	89%
Catalogs, lists, bibliographies	(18)	64

[1]The figures in parentheses indicate the number of respondents; the figures that follow represent that number as a percentage of all responses.

Table 5: Statistical Summary of Survey Responses (continued)

Local database development	(11)	39%
Remote database searching	(12)	43
Computer-assisted instruction	(8)	29
Local database searching	(8)	29
Circulation control/backup	(5)	18
Acquisitions	(1)	3
Interlibrary loan	(4)	14
Serials control	(2)	7
A/V control	(4)	14
Online catalog	(4)	14
Reserve book room	(2)	7

Microcomputer Ownership

Apple line (total)	(27)	96%
II+	(12)	43
IIe	(10)	36
II	(3)	11
Lisa	(1)	3
Macintosh	(1)	3
IBM line (total)	(11)	39%
PC/XT	(6)	21
PC	(4)	14
OCLC (modified)	(1)	3
TRS-80 line (total)	(8)	29%
Model II	(4)	14
Model III	(2)	7
Model 12	(1)	3
Model 100	(1)	3

PUBLIC LIBRARIES

Microcomputer Use
(25 Responses)

Is your library part of an integrated system?	no	(22)[1]	88%
	yes	(3)	12
Is your micro available for patron use?	no	(6)	24
	yes	(19)	76

[1]The figures in parentheses indicate the number of respondents; the figures that follow represent that number as a percentage of all responses.

Table 5: Statistical Summary of Survey Responses (continued)

Has your library developed its own software?	no	(12)	48%
	yes	(13)	52

Does your library expect to purchase additional software?	no	(2)	8
	yes	(22)	88
	unsure	(1)	4

Does your library expect to develop its own software?	no	(15)	60
	yes	(8)	32
	unsure	(2)	8

Applications

General management	(21)	84%
Catalogs, lists, bibliographies	(14)	56
Local database development	(11)	44
Remote database searching	(4)	16
Computer-assisted instruction	(10)	40
Local database searching	(4)	16
Circulation control/backup	(5)	20
Acquisitions	(8)	32
Interlibrary loan	(5)	20
Serials control	(4)	16
A/V control	(4)	16
Online catalog	(1)	4
Reserve book room	(0)	0

Microcomputer Ownership

Apple line (total)	(21)	84%
II+	(13)	52
IIe	(5)	20
II	(3)	12

IBM line (total)	(6)	24%
PC	(3)	12
PC/XT	(3)	12

TRS-80 line (total)	(12)	48%
Model II	(5)	20
Model III	(5)	20
Model 16	(1)	4
Model IV	(1)	4

Table 5: Statistical Summary of Survey Responses (continued)

SPECIAL LIBRARIES
(Government, Corporate, Medical)

Microcomputer Use
(11 Responses)

Is your micro part of an integrated system?	no	(9)[1]	82%
	yes	(2)	18
Is your micro available for patron use?	no	(8)	73
	yes	(3)	27
Has your library developed its own software?	no	(7)	64
	yes	(4)	36
Does your library expect to purchase additional software?	no	(1)	9
	yes	(9)	82
	unsure	(1)	9
Does your library expect to develop its own software?	no	(6)	55
	yes	(4)	36
	unsure	(1)	9

Applications

General management	(9)	82%
Catalogs, lists, bibliographies	(7)	64
Local database development	(8)	73
Remote database searching	(8)	73
Computer-assisted instruction	(2)	18
Local database searching	(4)	36
Circulation control/backup	(3)	27
Acquisitions	(2)	18
Interlibrary loan	(2)	18
Serials control	(3)	27
A/V control	(1)	9
Online catalog	(2)	18
Reserve book room	(0)	0

[1]The figures in parentheses indicate the number of respondents; the figures that follow represent that number as a percentage of all responses.

Table 5: Statistical Summary of Survey Responses (continued)

Microcomputer Ownership

Apple line (total)	(6)	55%
II+	(3)	27
IIe	(2)	18
II	(1)	9
IBM line (total)	(3)	27%
PC	(2)	18
OCLC (modified)	(1)	9
TRS-80 line (total)	(4)	36%
Model II	(3)	27
Model 12	(1)	9

Part III

Profiles of
Library Microcomputer Projects

BAPTIST HOSPITAL HEALTH SCIENCE LIBRARY
Miami, FL

Type of library: Medical
Size of population: 1600
Type of population: Hospital staff
Micros owned: 1 Apple II+
Software packages owned: PFS, PFS: Report, WordStar, Apple Writer
Software developed in-house: None
Languages supported: BASIC
Operating systems: DOS, CP/M

The microcomputer program at Baptist Hospital Health Science Library is "physician driven." The staff doctors provided both the financial support and encouragement that enabled the library to move into the microcomputer age. The library's Apple II+, which includes a printer, two disk drives and several software packages, was acquired through a donation by the Physicians Medical Fund. Total cost of the purchase was approximately $5000, and the additional software acquired since the original purchase in 1981 has also been covered by the Fund.

The microcomputer serves two general functions at the hospital—

the library staff uses it for different administrative applications, while the physicians use it for education and patient care. All use is supervised by head librarian Diane Ream. Prior to the acquisition, Ream had had no previous experience with micros per se. She was familiar with new technologies, however, because the hospital had been using a larger Texas Instruments computer for online medical searching for a number of years.

In implementing the microcomputer program the hospital had the support of the local Apple dealer as well as the aid of a doctor's wife who is an Apple consultant. The choice of the Apple was dictated largely by the availability of software designed to meet the needs of physicians.

In the library setting, Ream uses the micro, with WordStar software, primarily for word processing tasks such as correspondence, creation of the hospital newsletter and union list production. Ream has also experimented with tracking overdues with the Apple, but that program is not yet fully refined. PFS software is used for record keeping and has been particularly helpful in tracking statistics about online use. PFS was also used for a time to keep a record of the hospital's serials, but the project was abandoned because the PFS program was not big enough.

Doctors have full access to the micro and use it in the care of critical patients and in the development of nutrition programs. In addition, the doctors use the Apple for standard computer-assisted instruction (CAI) purposes, running different instructional programs. The library has also created a database for the doctors which tracks the medical credits each doctor has earned in continuing education work.

Ream reports that the Apple has done everything the library had expected of it, and has performed without any major equipment failures. The micro is kept in a stationary location and use is closely supervised by Ream.

CORDIS CORP. LIBRARY
Miami, FL

Type of library: Corporate
Size of population: 2500

Type of population: Corporate staff
Micros owned: 2 NCR Worksavers
Software packages owned: NCR software, DataTrek, dBase II
Software developed in-house: None
Languages supported: None
Operating systems: CP/M

Sharyn Ladner, librarian for Miami-based Cordis Corp., is une-quivocal in her response to the benefits microcomputers can provide for any type of library. "They allow us to do things we never have been able to do in the past," Ladner says. The company's micro has enabled the library to improve its online searching capabilities, as well as improve what Ladner calls "internal processing" functions.

The Cordis library uses the NCR Worksaver almost exclusively for online searching. Cordis subscribes to several databases, and the NCR has replaced a Texas Instruments computer in the searching process. The NCR permits the library to prepare "value-added" searches, Ladner explains. A value-added search is one in which extraneous material, such as the search strategy, can be edited out before the results of the search are presented to the patron. "Using the micro lets us present much cleaner, more professional looking searches," Ladner says. Micros also mean that searches can be printed out on a matrix printer (on eight-by-eleven paper), thereby ending the practice of printing on thermal paper (long rolls of computer printouts) and making the final documents easier to handle. In addition, the NCR allows the library to include a list of sources used for a search along with the results of the search.

In the first six months of using the micro for online searching the number of searches increased from approximately 150 per month to more than 200 per month. Ladner believes the increase in the number of searches is best explained by corporate growth, but the micro may have added to the increase by making the documents easier to read and manipulate. Using the micro has not increased the speed of the searches, as the library downloads all of its searches and the word processing function slows the search down slightly. No patrons are permitted to conduct searches and all requests are handled by Ladner.

Many of the internal processing functions are still in the planning stages, although some parts (interlibrary loan, acquisitions, database development and circulation control) were implemented in winter 1984. These functions are run using dBase II software. The library uses the NCR for book ordering. The library orders books for several departments within the company, and the micro allows the library to keep track of what books have been ordered by what departments and/or individuals. Closer monitoring of the book ordering process has enabled the library to reduce duplication of orders and to start a charge-back system with the departments that acquired the materials.

In spring 1984 the Cordis library acquired DataTrek software with the goal of beginning to computerize its serials operations, particularly checkin and routing procedures. Ladner is designing the programs with help from the company's computer experts. Another application Cordis hopes to implement in the future is electronic mail. At present the two NCRs are only networked with each other, but when the company begins its electronic mail system, plans call for the library's micros to be integrated with it.

It was the planned integration of the library's micros with the company's other machines that was the determining factor in acquiring an NCR for the library. "The NCR is the company computer," Ladner says, noting that she had no choice but to order that brand of micro. Although the NCR has performed well, Ladner thinks the NCR is "more expensive than it is useful." The biggest drawback of the NCR is the lack of software for library functions, Ladner complains. Most of the software the library uses came packaged with the hardware, although Ladner has modified some programs for more specific uses. If Ladner had her choice she would choose an IBM PC/XT for the library, largely because of the greater amount of software available.

Despite the drawbacks of the NCR, the micro has proved an invaluable aid to the corporate library. "Without the micros we could not even think of doing any kind of automation," Ladner says, noting that the cost of automating with a mini or mainframe computer would be prohibitive for a library of Cordis's size. (The library has two professional staff members and two clerical assistants.) The micros, however, allowed Cordis to computerize its operations for under $25,000.

Because it is part of a larger corporation, some of the library's costs of implementing the micro system have been minimized. The maintenance contract of the library's micro is included as part of the total company contract, and includes software upgrades. The corporate word processing staff trained the library staff on the different word processing capabilities of the micro. For training on the searches, staff members attended classes conducted by Dialog, and Ladner continues to attend seminars on searching.

DENVER PUBLIC LIBRARY
Denver, CO

Type of Library: Public
Size of population: 495,000
Type of population: General public
Micros owned: 2 Apple IIes, 3 Apple II+s, 1 IBM PC/XT
Software packages owned: PFS, PFS: Report, VisiCalc, Bank Street
    Writer, Apple Writer, Word Juggler, dBase II
Software developed in-house: Donor Record
Languages supported: BASIC
Operating systems: DOS 2.2, DOS 3.3, ProDOS 1.1, DOS 3.3 (Apple)

Patron use and office automation have been the two primary applications of microcomputers in the Denver Public Library System. There are a total of six microcomputers in use systemwide, serving several different functions.

Three Apple II+ machines are located at three separate Denver branch libraries. The micros, which have 64K memory, a DOS 3.3 operating system and an Epson dot matrix printer, are owned by a local entrepreneur—as is the accompanying software. The Apples are permanently attached to a security table, and there is a $4 per hour charge for patron use. Although the library derives no profit from the arrangement, it does provide a service to the public at no cost to the library. The library arranged for the third-party service by issuing an RFP (request for a proposal). Any company interested in a for-profit microcomputer venture could submit a bid to the library. Since only one local firm responded with a proposal for the venture, the library accepted its bid.

This lack of enthusiasm was something of a precursor of things to come. The patron program has not yet lived up to the expectations of either the library or the vendor. It is hoped that newly rejuvenated training sessions will help to spur interest. Formerly conducted on an ad hoc basis, classes are now scheduled regularly and taught by a former library staff member. The classes offer instruction on the micros using VisiCalc, PFS and PFS: Report software. The sessions are priced at $20.

Although response to the patron use program has not been as great as hoped, there has been enough interest for one Denver branch library to spend special trust-fund dollars to acquire its own micro, an Apple

IIe with 128K memory, DOS 3.3 operating system and an Okidata printer. The library borrowed money from a special trust fund and will repay the $2000 price from monies generated by renting time on the micro to the public. The branch library has also acquired some PFS, PFS: Report and VisiCalc software packages, which will be used for administrative word processing as well as to monitor patron use of the micro.

The Denver system's marketing and accounting departments have their own micros—an IBM PC/XT for the marketing department and an Apple IIe for the accounting department. The $4800 IBM features 128K RAM memory, a DOS 2.2 operating system plus an Epson printer, while the $3500 Apple IIe also includes 128K RAM memory, an Epson printer and Apple DOS 3.3 operating system. The marketing department, under the direction of Jim Everett, marketing manager, has developed its own software package, Donor Record. The program is a maintenance system used to record library donors and for such purposes as generating mailing lists. The accounting department primarily uses its Apple IIe for cost accounting. The library has also created a database which monitors personnel data such as employee leave, insurance and pay grades.

Denver's micro applications are coordinated by systems analyst Bill Campbell and director of computer operations Ruth Rosenfield. Mixing Apples and IBMs is not something that Campbell worries about. The library was not concerned about the compatibility of its early micros, since its initial goal was not to develop an integrated network system. The Denver library is more interested in familiarizing its staff with microcomputers and in meeting some immediate needs. Staff attitude toward the machines has steadily improved as personnel have gained more experience with the micros. Training is conducted on an informal basis; staff members are encouraged to attend the training sessions conducted by the library for the general public, and the library has periodically conducted evening training sessions of eight weeks for staff and patrons.

Although both Rosenfield and Campbell oversee the microcomputer operation, the library has not yet established any standardized procedures with regard to its computer program. Rosenfield and Campbell monitor the operation as part of their other duties, troubleshooting problems and answering technical questions when they arise. Campbell also was involved in choosing the Apple IIe for the branch library, acting as the library's computer expert.

The most ambitious use of micros at Denver is yet to come. The system recently completed a review and selection process, and expects to acquire six or seven Wangs for administrative purposes. The system will consist of the Wangs networked together with a minicomputer and will be used by the administrative offices.

GRACE A. DOW MEMORIAL LIBRARY
Midland, MI

Type of library: Public
Size of population: 73,500
Type of population: General public
Micros owned: 1 Apple II+, 1 Franklin 1000
Software packages owned: Screen Writer, VisiCalc, Bank Street Writer,
    Data Reporter, PFS: Report
Software developed in-house: None
Languages supported: BASIC, PASCAL
Operating systems: DOS 3.3

Staff use of microcomputers has taken something of a backseat to a public access program at the Grace A. Dow Memorial Library. The library's two micros—an Apple II+ and a Franklin 1000—are both available for patron and administrative use. To avoid conflicts with the public, the staff does the bulk of its work on the micros either in the morning before the library opens, or on days when the public use of the micros is light. If a staff member wishes to use one of the machines when public use is heavy he or she must reserve time like any patron. Although Randall Dykhuis, reference librarian, says this arrangement has caused few problems, the library has ordered an IBM PC solely for use by the library staff.

The most frequent use of the micros by the staff is for word processing applications. Screen Writer is used to generate mailing lists, write reports and letters, and for other writing tasks. Another important use of the micro has been in an interlibrary loan program, which was begun in spring 1984. Dow's Apple hooks the branch library to its headquarters in Saginaw, where all of its loan requests are sent. Each request is then transmitted to the library that has the needed book. The interlibrary loan program is operated each morning by a part-time staff member who was trained on the micro by the library's user services supervisor. Although the program has not been fully evaluated, early indications are that it has quickened the delivery of books from other libraries.

Data Reporter is the software used for the library's database management functions. The library is using this program to update its videocassette holdings, and to index the local paper. The micros allow patrons to search the paper index by name of article, subject or date. This has permitted the library to try some projects it was unable to do in the past, such as a genealogy indexing all the local obituaries back to the 1800s. The library also owns the PFS: Report management system, but has yet to use the program due to a lack of staff time to explore its capabilities.

Lack of staff time is also preventing Dow from implementing as many micro applications as it would like. As the micro program has operated in the past, staff use has been very uneven, with some librarians using the micros quite a bit and others not at all. When the IBM is up and running, Dow hopes to be able to train more staff members on the micros. Dow is not buying the new IBM for the purpose of adding new applications, but will be using it for the same purposes as its other computers. Hopefully, new applications can gradually be added. Dykhuis acknowledges that the incompatibility of the IBM with the Apple and the Franklin could cause some problems. Dykhuis, who acquires the software for the library, was not in on the decision to acquire the IBM, which was made by the library director. That decision was largely based on the ability to get a "good price on the IBM," Dykhuis says.

While the administrative use of micros still has some bugs to be ironed out, the library has been pleased with its public access program. Dow introduced the program in spring 1982 using an Apple II+ and added the Franklin in 1983. Patrons receive a 20-minute orientation program on the mechanics of the machine the first time they use the micros. Dow keeps no record of which patrons have taken part in the orientation, instead relying on trust and observation. The library trusts that its patrons will honor its orientation policy without being checked up on. Patrons who have not taken the orientation course can usually be spotted by the library staff, as they tend to adopt a confused look rather quickly, Dykhuis says.

Patrons are urged to sign up in advance to reserve time on the micros. Reservations can be booked in one-half to two hour time blocks and there is a $2 per hour charge. Price for students (through college) is $1 per hour. Children under 14 must be accompanied by an adult. Dow reports that there has been little resistance to the micro charge. In addition to generating revenue, the fee ensures that only people who are seriously interested in learning about micros will use the machines. A Canon electric typewriter is available to use as a printer with both micros, using either Data Reporter or Screen Writer. Dow also makes floppy disks available for sale. The only negative experience Dow has had in its public access program involved the loaning of software. Dow's attempt to circulate software failed, as many disks were returned damaged or unworkable.

The library's software collection is divided into two areas—copyrighted programs and public domain programs. All public domain programs can be used at the library or copied for home use, while copyrighted materials may only be used at the library. Dow buys few software programs specifically for patron use, and no game packages. Instead, the library purchases programs that can be used by both staff and patrons. The library has an annual software budget of about $1100. Dow has also been able to supplement these holdings with donations, particularly from the local and national Apple Clubs. The Midland, MI Apple Club has also provided the library with evaluations and recommendations of software. The club uses the library's Apple II+ on the one Saturday evening per month they meet at the library.

Donations played an important part in the acquisition of Dow's hardware as well. Both the Apple and the Franklin were acquired following donations from several different parties. Expenditures on the hardware have been about $3500.

EAST CAROLINA UNIVERSITY
Health Sciences Library
Greenville, NC

Type of library: University
Size of population: 4000

Type of population: Faculty, students
Micros owned: 3 TRS-80 Model IIs, 2 TRS-80 Model 12s, 3 Apple IIes
Software packages owned: dBase II, Scripsit, VisiCalc, CrossTalk
Software developed in-house: Reserve control system, Spine label
    generation program, Interlibrary loan program
Languages supported: BASIC
Operating systems: DOS

The Health Sciences Library at East Carolina University has eight microcomputers of which the three TRS-80 Model IIs are used primarily for library applications. One Model II has a single disk drive, a second has two disk drives and a third has three disk drives as well as expanded memory. East Carolina first began using micros in 1980 and since then has steadily increased the number of tasks being performed by the machines.

Like many other libraries, East Carolina's micro experience started with word processing. For word processing applications the university uses Scripsit software. Scripsit was chosen because it allows documents to be quickly and easily edited and it can be easily learned. Using Scripsit, East Carolina produces its policy, procedure and orientation manuals. In each case, the manual is divided into logical segments so that each segment can be produced separately. This is done for two reasons. First, it means that as segments are revised it will not be necessary to reproduce the entire manual, only those segments that have been changed. Second, by dividing the manual into sections, the library guards against the possibility of losing the whole work if the power fails or the program malfunctions.

The use of the word processor has greatly reduced the amount of time spent in revisions. When East Carolina revised its policy manual in the past, at least 30 of the 60 pages had to be retyped, even though only minor revisions were necessary. The word processor has eliminated the unnecessary typing, thereby allowing for the development of more current manuals.

In addition to producing operating manuals, the word processor is being used to produce all of East Carolina's correspondence, annual and quarterly reports, job descriptions, performance objectives, user education guides and mailing lists. A daisy wheel printer gives the library excellent mimeograph stencils, enabling it to produce certain materials which otherwise would have to be sent to an outside firm.

East Carolina used Profile software to create an equipment inventory system. With the program, an East Carolina staff member simply has to select the function that is desired and type that number. For example, if a staff member wants to record a new piece of equipment the number seven would be typed. The equipment can then be identified by a variety of methods including inventory control number, the university control number, description of equipment and room number locations. Using the database, East Carolina is then able to produce monthly equipment inventory lists for each department within the library.

Although Profile has been a success in the creation of the equipment inventory, it proved to be unsuitable in the development of a reserve record system. The goal of the project was to create a system whereby the staff could input data and then quickly and easily identify all the items on reserve for a particular course. Profile proved unsatisfactory because it required too much processing space, and with only two disk drives (at the time) East Carolina was unable to enter all its reserve items.

Since the Profile software was unable to meet East Carolina's needs, the library chose to have someone on campus write a program specifically for its requirements. As outlined by the library administration the reserve control system is to include the following functions:

1. Maintain a file of all items faculty want to place on reserve;
2. Maintain a number of bibliographic data elements for each reserve item and maintain other identification information such as the course name, instructor's name and term during which the item is to be placed on reserve;
3. Permit the reserve assistant to quickly determine if the requested item is already in the file, and to determine if it is currently on reserve;
4. Produce a list which can be produced alphabetically by author, classification number, course and instructor of all items to be placed on reserve in a given term;
5. Produce a list of all items which have been requested for reserve, but are not on reserve already. The list must be able to be produced alphabetically by title, and journals must be listed separately from books;
6. Produce lists by course number to be used as locational devices for students and to be sent to faculty for review.

To meet these varied requirements East Carolina developed a program using dBase II, Vedit and QuickCode. The secret to success has been that these programs offer flexibility to meet all the reserve room control needs. Using its TRS-80 with three disk drives and expanded memory, East Carolina has successfully placed most of its reserves into the main database. Although East Carolina has viewed the reserve control program generally as a success, the problem of processing space and storage still remains.

In addition to the customized reserve room system, East Carolina has produced two other programs in-house. One program is used in conjunction with the OCLC terminal to produce spine labels for books. When East Carolina is producing its cards on OCLC, the library requests the label format on OCLC and instructs the OCLC terminal to transfer the label format to the micro in an abbreviated form. This procedure is repeated for each book as the cataloging information is edited. When the editing is finished, the labels are printed on pressure sensitive labels.

A more ambitious program is East Carolina's interlibrary loan program. When processing an interlibrary loan East Carolina uses dBase commands to get the formatted screen which is used to enter the interlibrary loan information. The operator types the required information (patron, department, identification number, date requested, form, title, author, verification) on the screen. After one request is completed the information for the next loan is entered. After the information is entered for all library loans to be done that day, the operator requests the print mode. The loan request forms are printed one by one at which point the program checks the journal database for copyright compliance.

To close a loan once it is received, the operator requests the edit mode and enters the record number of the loan desired, the date the item was received, the filling library, the cost of the loan and a "Y" to indicate the transaction was completed.

The East Carolina loan program also produces a number of reports: lists of requests by patrons, overdue letters, notices to users to remind them of due dates and resubmission requests. Monthly statistics produced include a list of requests by department, the cost per department, total number of requests left in the pending file, the number of requests completed and length of time it took the request to be filled. At the end of the year East Carolina receives a list of journal titles and the number of times it tried to request each title.

A final application is maintenance of statistical information. VisiCalc is used to maintain a statistical database on all East Carolina's library operations. The program enables the library to manipulate its data to respond to the different types of requests it constantly receives.

Although East Carolina was reluctant to discuss financial information, a spokesman estimated that the basic equipment for a TRS-80 Model II with two disk drives, a letter quality printer and the basic software (Scripsit, Profile and VisiCalc) cost approximately $7000. It took approximately five days to learn Scripsit, two and one-half days to learn Profile and a half day for label maker.

EKSTROM LIBRARY
University of Louisville
Louisville, KY

Type of library: University
Size of population: 20,000
Type of population: Students, faculty, community
Micros owned: 2 Apple II+s, 1 IBM PC/XT
Software packages owned: PFS: File, PFS: Report, Apple Writer II,
    VisiFile, Hartley Create: Lessons, dBase II, WordStar, QuickCode
Software developed in-house: None
Languages supported: BASIC
Operating systems: DOS 3.3, PC DOS

The microcomputer program at the Ekstrom Library on the University of Louisville campus started with a modest investment in software for a demonstration library project at the university's main computer center. Only when the demonstration proved successful did the library commit itself to purchasing its own machines. The library owns three micros, with the Apple II+s used for the most diverse applications.

Convinced of the value of micros, Sharon Edge, head of library circulation, encouraged her supervisor to acquire one. Her supervisor, David Reed, was in turn able to get library funds approved for the purchase of two PFS software packages. After the successful demonstration of a reserve system program mentioned above, the library approved the purchase of an Apple II+, including two disk drives, a 12-inch monitor, Epson MX-100 printer, and interface card and cable. Cost of the acquisition was $3200.

Since its acquisition in 1982 the Apple has been in almost constant use, serving database management, word processing, electronic spreadsheet and CAI functions.

As a database management tool the Apple is used in three ways—to monitor the course reserve collection, generate late notices and maintain records for enclosed study carrels.

In order to monitor the course reserve collection the library prints out each book list by professor's name and by author and title. Ekstrom chose PFS: File and PFS: Report software for these functions, primarily because PFS is easy to learn and use.

PFS software is also used to generate late notices to borrowers. Because the circulation department did not have access to word processing software, PFS (normally used only for database management applications) was adapted for use in word processing tasks. The text in each notice remained the same while the following items were set up as the data elements on the blank form to be filled in whenever a notice needed to be sent: name, address and library card number of the borrower; date of notice and date recall fine begins; call number, title and OCR number of recalled volume. Because the data are entered into a database management system, there is the added capability of being able to print reports sorted on any data element (such as name or address).

PFS software packages are also used in a third database management function, the maintenance of records for enclosed study carrels. Here records are kept monitoring which students are assigned to which carrels, expiration dates and infractions of policies. The chief benefit of this application is the ability to sort records by any data element included in the record.

Ekstrom selected Apple Writer II to conduct its word processing chores. Chief factors in the selection of Apple Writer II were its ease of use and the availability of other professionals on campus who could be consulted if problems arose. Apple Writer II has been most efficiently used in tasks which require frequent or extensive revision.

For the electronic spreadsheet function, the circulation department chose VisiCalc. The department uses VisiCalc to monitor the student wage budget and to compile statistics for annual reports and other management needs. Using the micro allows the department to automatically recalculate totals when new figures are added or old figures changed.

The circulation department also uses the micros for computer-assisted instruction. Using Hartley Courseware's Create: Lessons the circulation department has created programs to train students in library procedures. In less than one week the library staff created programs on charging out books, placing holds and placing call numbers in order. Student library workers are thus able to learn various library tasks at their leisure while the library staff is able to concentrate on matters other than training student workers.

Use of micros is not limited to the circulation department. The University of Louisville Photographic Archives unit acquired an IBM PC/XT in 1983. The incentive to purchase the micro was provided when the university decided to scrap its DEC-10 mainframe computer. The archives department had used the mainframe to provide access to its collection of more than 800,000 photographs and manuscripts. Because the archive unit will not be able to use the machine replacing the DEC, a search for alternatives was undertaken. With the purchase of the IBM the archives unit has begun to produce its own finding aids, such as lists and indexes, using dBase II. The unit has produced both a master record for one collection, and, from that master, indexes. Cost of the IBM was $7000 and included extra memory, boards, monitor, printer, software, service contracts and hard disk.

The acquisitions department of the Ekstrom Library also uses a micro. The equipment is another Apple II+, purchased as part of an acquisitions system from Gaylord Bros., Inc. The micro performs all acquisition functions including online ordering, receiving and bookkeeping.

The Gaylord system, including the Apple, was acquired as a stopgap measure until the library is able to get funds to acquire an integrated system that will perform all library functions, including acquisition and circulation. Initially, Ekstrom reported a number of bugs with the Gaylord system, but the problems were resolved by the vendor.

Despite the significant amount of micro use at the Ekstrom Library the university has no centrally administered plan for either acquiring micros or for training staff. The micros owned by the library were acquired as a result of individual initiative, particularly in the case of the circulation and archives department purchases. Similarly, the training of the library staff has, to date, been conducted on an ad hoc basis. Library officials realize that if micros are to be used more efficiently, a central operating plan is necessary. David Reed is lobbying for such a plan, which would encompass procedures for micro purchases and training. His immediate goal is to develop a program that will allow more staff members to use the library micros more efficiently for routine tasks.

FAIRPORT PUBLIC LIBRARY
Fairport, NY

Type of library: Public
Size of population: 24,000
Type of population: General public
Micros owned: 1 Apple II+
Software packages owned: Games
Software developed in-house: Work schedule for student pages
Languages supported: BASIC, PASCAL, LOGO
Operating systems: DOS 3.3

The Fairport Public Library had two motives in mind when it initiated its public access microcomputer program in October 1980. First, the library wanted to familiarize its staff with a computer before the installation of a computerized circulation system to be instituted throughout the Monroe County library system. Second, the library wanted to promote computer literacy in the community through a hands-on computer program. By the summer of 1984 Fairport Public felt it had achieved both of its goals.

The focus of the micro program is an Apple II+ that the library acquired with funds provided by a grant from the Monroe County library system and a donation from the Friends of the Library. The cost of the original computer was $1495 and the library also acquired a language card system for $495 as well as a second disk drive in 1981 for $595. The Apple was selected for the project because the Fairport public school system used an Apple in its schools, and the library wanted its program to be compatible with that of the schools.

However, the library's public access program is intended for the entire community, not just students. The library estimates that approximately half of the participants in the program are adults. Any interested computer user, regardless of age, must first take a one-hour computer orientation program. At the start of the program in 1980, five orientation sessions per week were held, with 15 people per session. That number has since dropped to approximately 10 people per week taking the course. The sessions are conducted by different Fairport staff members on a rotating basis. Computer users do not have to be Fairport residents or have a library card, but Fairport does maintain a list of the people who have taken the orientation session, and no one is allowed to use the computer until they have completed the free course.

Patrons are restricted to one hour of computer time per week. Time slots can be reserved by calling the library and can be booked in 30-minute blocks. The library has two types of time slots, "free time" which is for game playing, and "for programming only" which is for practicing programming, homework or educational games. Fairport reports that the computer is usually booked solid on weekday afternoons and all day on Saturdays. The library estimates that the Apple is in use about 10 hours a day.

Fairport has an annual budget of $1900 for the purchase of micro software. Its software collection consists of arcade-type games, math and business applications, tutorials, instructions on how to program and educational games. Fairport reports that the arcade-type programs are the most popular with an estimated 60% of the computer users preferring these programs. The use of programming software has increased markedly since the micro program began, while math and business applications software are the least popular. Fairport keeps a master copy of every diskette and only duplicates are available for patron use. When a disk wears out, a new one can easily be made from the master.

The acceptance of the micro program has been overwhelmingly favorable, with no public cries that the service is an unneeded frill. The library has received a great amount of local press coverage about the program, thereby increasing its visibility in the community. Fairport is also certain that the addition of this program has helped to attract people who had never used the library before.

Fairport admits that at the beginning the micro program was an extremely time-consuming endeavor. However, once the library had established set procedures for using the micro, the time burden was eased. A time study completed in January 1982 indicated only five and one-half hours of staff time was devoted to the computer that month and four and one-half hours of that time was spent on giving orientation classes to patrons. The Fairport library staff offered little resistance to the micro program. Each staff member attended a 20 hour in-service training course offered by the Fairport high school math department, which helped staff members familiarize themselves with the capabilities of a computer.

As successful as the public access program has been, Fairport has no immediate plans to add administrative applications. At present the library uses the Apple for only one library task. The senior clerk uses the micro to do the work schedules for the library's pages. The schedule took the clerk a full day to complete when it was done manually. Using the Apple, however, the schedule can be finished in 20 minutes.

CLEMENT C. FRY COLLECTION
Yale Medical Library
New Haven, CT

Type of library: Medical
Size of population: 150
Type of population: Yale faculty and students, researchers
Micros owned: 1 North Star Horizon, 1 IBM PC/XT
Software packages owned: WordStar
Software developed in-house: Microbase
Languages supported: FORTRAN, BASIC
Operating systems: CP/M, H DOS

"A 100-fold increase in the use of the collection," was the outcome of the Yale Medical Library's Clement C. Fry Collection microbased project. The project features a specially designed system that combines microcomputer and microfiche technologies. The aim of the Fry Collection Project, as envisioned by librarian Susan Wheeler, was to develop a system that would manage the 2000-item medical art collection more efficiently, and create a practical, low-cost method for creating full access to the collection. To meet this goal, Wheeler, in collaboration with Dr. David Stagg, director of the Yale biomedical computing unit, and William Guth, director of communications media, Yale University School of Medicine, initiated the Fry micro project in late 1979.

The system features Microbase, a database management system developed and written specifically for the Fry Collection Project by Dr. Stagg. Microbase catalogs the 2000 printings and drawings of the Fry Collection on a North Star Horizon micro with 64K memory and an 18 megabyte Winchester hard disk drive. Microbase features include a user-defined format of up to 117 fields, variable length fields, fast searching of each field and user friendliness. Microbase is run with four commands and operates under CP/M. Catalog entries are prepared with a text editor. WordStar software is used in conjunction with the program to type in all database information.

The printings and drawings, which relate to the history of medicine from the 15th to the 20th century, are cataloged according to 43 categories arranged in 32 fields. A print or drawing and/or its catalog entry can be retrieved by searching any one of the fields. A subject authority file of approximately 550 terms was systematically generated from the database during the cataloging process.

The micro catalog is designed to be used in conjunction with color microfiche. The method for producing single-copy color microfiche was devised by William Guth. The two access systems, visual and informational, sit side by side on a table top and are used by patrons and researchers. Catalog entries, as well as various indexes, are available in hard copy. However, all catalog searching is done by computer, which prints out the results in a standardized format. The librarian can then rearrange this data as needed, to provide customized responses in printed form.

The management system has provided two distinct benefits. As mentioned above, the system has greatly increased the use of the Fry Collection by both Yale personnel and by outside researchers. The increased usage has been attributed to the greater accessibility to the collection that the system provides. The system is extremely user-friendly, and Wheeler is on hand to assist anyone who may have trouble. In fact, although the system is designed so that anyone can use the program, it is Wheeler who conducts most of the searches.

The librarians also benefit from the system. The management system allows for more detailed cataloging and the collection's holdings can be continually updated. In addition, the library staff is better able to monitor the collection and is able to locate any particular piece of material at any given time.

Funding for the Fry Collection Project was provided by a corporate gift from Hoffmann-LaRoche. The grant covered the $10,000 cost of the North Star Horizon and an Epson MX-80 printer. Wheeler reports no major problems with either the software or hardware.

Despite the success of the Fry project, there is little likelihood that micro applications will soon spread throughout the Yale Medical Library. There is "tremendous resistance" to the use of micros at the library by staff members, who are inflicted by "mainframe mentality," Wheeler says. Most staff members at the library are used to purchasing a complete database service, such as Medline, and the concept of creating their own database does not take hold, Wheeler explains. In February 1984 the medical library acquired its second micro, an IBM PC/XT, which had not been put to use by the summer of that year.

A final note: The Microbase system (copyrighted by Dr. Stagg) is available for sale. Price for the program is $1000.

GLENDORA LIBRARY AND CULTURAL CENTER
Glendora, CA

Type of library: Public
Size of population: 40,000
Type of population: General public
Micros owned: 2 IBM PCs, 1 IBM PC/XT, 1 TRS-80 Model III, 1 Apple IIe, 2 Eagle 1600s
Software packages owned: dBase II, Lotus 1-2-3, CrossTalk, WordStar, Perfect Writer
Software developed in-house: Circulation program
Languages supported: BASIC, PASCAL
Operating systems: DOS, CP/M, CP/M 86

The microcomputer program at the Glendora Library has its roots in Proposition 13. The budget cutbacks that followed the passage of the proposition provided Glendora head librarian John Jolly with an unexpected amount of free time, time Jolly used to acquire a TRS-80 Model I micro (this micro was eventually replaced by a Model III). Having taken some computer programming courses, Jolly, with the help of a computer consultant, began writing programs for the TRS-80 in an effort to ease the fears of librarians about micros as well as to demonstrate the cost-saving potential the machines represented.

Jolly's first programs allowed Glendora to print full sets of card catalogs with the TRS-80. Meanwhile, staff members began experimenting with different ways the micro could help them in their jobs. Word processing applications were the most popular. After Jolly and the rest of the staff became more comfortable with the concept of using micros, Jolly developed a sample circulation control system. The sample system, which Jolly wrote using dBase II software, proved extremely effective, and in summer 1984 Glendora installed a permanent IBM micro-based circulation system.

The Glendora system encompasses all aspects of the circulation process. To be run in conjunction with the library's IBM micros, the system automatically checks materials in and out, computes fines, prepares overdue notices, prepares bills and processes reserves. In addition, programs are provided for processing new acquisitions of books, AV materials, periodicals and for adding new borrowers to the files. Delinquent borrowers are blocked at checkout time, although an operator can override this command.

Barcodes are used to identify both patrons and library materials. Numbers are read into the system using either standard barcode label-reading equipment or by the operator at the console. The Codabar labels have a check digit which is verified by the system to keep errors to a minimum.

Checkouts are processed by reading the barcode of the patron and the barcodes of the items to be checked out. The system will display overdue book titles and amount of fines owed by the patron. Checkins are also processed by reading the barcode of the item. Any fines are automatically computed and can be billed to the patron at the operator's option. If the item is on reserve complete information about the requestor is displayed.

As developed by Jolly, the system operates on CP/M and CP/M 86 operating systems. The system functions are accessed through a menu screen which guides the operator to the desired function. The menu and input screens are self explanatory, providing for quick operator training. Jolly has trained the Glendora staff himself, and he reports that the librarians have been very receptive to the micro. All librarians at the circulation desk are capable of using the micro system.

In addition to the circulation system, Glendora has developed a simple book-ordering system and also uses its IBMs to maintain the monthly community activities calendar.

The micros have also provided some unexpected benefits to the library. Glendora uses an IBM to conduct its quarterly survey of patrons. The survey, mandated by the California State Library, tracks where the patrons of the library live. Previously Glendora would conduct the survey manually, a time-consuming process. With the micro, however, the report can be quickly totaled automatically by the IBM. The library has also benefitted from the micros with respect to its report for the county. In order to be reimbursed by the county for use of the library by county borrowers, Glendora must file a year-end report. Until this year the library would sort and type registration cards of some 2600 county borrowers. However, with the patron information collected by the circulation system, the list of county borrowers can be typed out by the computer, again saving a significant amount of time.

Glendora also has on hand two coin-operated micros for patron use. In operation since summer 1983, the charge for one half hour of use on the Apple IIe or TRS-80 Model III is 25 cents. Although the micro is popular, especially among young people, Glendora "still hasn't gotten its act together" on the most effective way to make the micros available for the patrons, Jolly says.

Jolly was unable to place a figure on how much the library has spent on micro hardware, in part because Glendora was able to obtain some micros from other city agencies that were no longer interested in the equipment. Similarly, the library has tried, unsuccessfully, to give its Eagle 1600 machines to other city departments. Since no agency has expressed an interest in receiving the Eagles, Jolly hopes to be able to find some applications for them at the library.

A portion of the funds for acquiring new hardware equipment is made available through regular library budget requests. Other monies have been generated by surpluses in other parts of the Glendora city budget. Purchases are made through the city's finance office with Jolly actively participating in the decisions. The library has no specific budget for software purchases, but because Jolly has written a number of programs, the software budget has been kept to a minimum, about $1000. Maintenance has yet to be a problem, with minor repairs handled by a local dealer.

MONROE C. GUTMAN LIBRARY
Harvard University Graduate School of Education
Cambridge, MA

Type of library: University
Size of population: 700
Type of population: Faculty, graduate education students
Micros owned: 3 Apple IIes, 3 Apple II+s, 1 Digital Rainbow 100 (on loan)
Software packages owned: WordStar, VisiCalc, PFS
Software developed in-house: None
Languages supported: BASIC
Operating systems: CP/M, DOS

Microcomputers play three very distinct roles at Harvard's Monroe C. Gutman Library. The Apple IIes and Apple II+s are used for administrative purposes, while a Digital Rainbow 100 micro is used in the development of an online edition of a library-created directory about micros in education. The Gutman Library Media Center has also developed a software archive and a micro hardware examination facility it calls the Software and Hardware Examination Collection.

This collection includes more than 20 state-of-the-art micros including Apple, Atari, Commodore, Digital, IBM, Radio Shack and Texas Instruments machines. All micros in the collection were donated to Monroe. The software section features more than 1000 programs, ranging from games to educational programs. The collection is open at no charge to graduate school faculty and students, alumni and some Cambridge area educational institutions. The library's policy of opening the collection to other outside parties is currently under review. The existing policy calls for visitors to pay a modest fee to examine the collection; visitors can only view the collection by prior arrangement.

The goal of the collection, which was started in 1982, is to provide a central place where the capabilities of different hardware and software materials can be examined. The library makes no recommendations or judgments regarding the qualities of one micro or software package compared to the others.

The Digital Rainbow 100, which is actually on loan to the library, is being used to create a national database of Microcomputer Applications in Education. Money for the project comes from the Fund for the Improvement of Postsecondary Education. The completed database and additional information in print form will supplement and eventually replace the library's earlier publication, *Directory of Microcomputer Applications in Education*. The directory will give details on what different institutes of higher education are doing with microcomputers.

The library's Apples are used primarily for word processing applications. Using mostly WordStar software, the library prepares mailing lists and writes articles and correspondence on the Apples. Barbara Graham, director of library media services, says word processing has allowed the library to operate efficiently despite a reduction in staff. Graham also notes that the micros will eventually enable the library to compile and analyze data better than ever before. The library has been using VisiCalc for this purpose, but only in a limited way until now. The library's media center uses the Apples with PFS software for inventory control, for cataloging its software collection and for preparing bibliographies.

Graham estimates that the library's micros are used an average of six hours per day, with no serious breakdown in operations. All staff members are encouraged to use the micros, and staff reception has been very positive. "The staff has recognized the value of micros as tools to make their jobs easier," Graham reports. Following the purchase of the micros the library held a series of "staff days," when the fundamentals of micros were taught. Other library administrators had earlier attended 16 hours of training sessions divided into four hour periods. The different training sessions helped make the introduction of micros into the library a relatively smooth process.

HERSHEY FOODS CORP. COMMUNICATIONS CENTER
Hershey, PA

Type of library: Corporate
Size of population: 250 in-house scientists, plus entire company
Type of population: Scientists, research and development staff, corporate management
Micros owned: Hewlett-Packard-125, IBM PC, OCLC 300
Software packages owned: VisiCalc, Word125, Graphics, Basic, Condor II, Link 125, The Micro Link II

Software developed in-house: None
Languages supported: BASIC
Operating systems: CP/M, DOS

Political as well as practical considerations played an important role in the Hershey Communications Center's move into microcomputers and its choice of the Hewlett-Packard-125. The chief proponent of micros was William Woodruff, head of the company's communications center, who felt that entering the micro age would improve the corporate image of the library. Woodruff's background in computers convinced him that the new technologies could also provide important benefits to corporate libraries. After reading the literature that was available about micros in 1980, particularly *Online*, Woodruff felt the HP-125 was the micro that could best meet the needs of the Hershey library.

Other factors favoring the HP-125 included the presence of other HP micros at Hershey, which gave the communications staff an opportunity to learn what functions the HP was capable of performing. In addition, the library was looking for a micro that could easily "talk" to the company's larger HP-1000. The Link 125 software provided easy communication with the HP-1000.

Originally, the primary function of the HP-125 was to "enhance the marketing features" of the communications center, according to Woodruff, and this application has remained the HP's chief function. The HP allows the library to present corporate personnel (executives, scientists, or research and development people) who have requested information a much more polished, finished product. Instead of providing reams of loose, thermal paper, the HP permits the communications center to create a more "glossy," complete package, thus helping to enhance the services that the center can provide, Woodruff believes. In addition, because of the speed of the HP, searches are performed more quickly and the center can provide a patron with some preliminary data immediately, and more detailed information at a later date.

Another benefit of the micro is the reduction in the amount of paper the center uses as well as a cutback on the large amount of copying. The center also uses the word processing capabilities of the HP to edit search results, thereby enhancing the completed materials.

The software that is used in the searching process is all developed specifically for the HP. Although Woodruff concedes he likes to "dabble" with the creation of different programs, he believes that it is more cost-effective to acquire commercial packages than to develop in-house programs. This applies not only to searching programs but to other applications as well.

For example, a growing application at Hershey has been the creation of small in-house databases. Using Condor II software, information is recorded by entering key words; then indexes of materials on specific subjects are printed. This is done most often in conjunction with the company's research and development department. The increasing use of the HP for database development is such that the company acquired a Winchester drive to hold its growing number of database file structures.

Hershey is also trying to modify its circulation system with the aid of the HP. Again using Condor software, the center has created a system where a list of overdues, represented by code numbers, is produced once a week. An overdue notice is then merged with a letter and sent to the patron. (As in most corporate libraries, however, circulation control is a relatively low priority for the Hershey library.) Using VisiCalc software, the center's administration office has done some statistical work with the HP.

The micro is used on the average of six hours per day. All of the center's staff has access to the machine, but no patron use is permitted. The HP has proved successful enough to justify the purchase of a second micro: the IBM PC, OCLC 300. It is hoped that the IBM will take some of the pressure off the usage of the HP. Initial plans call for using IBM in an interlibrary loan system with nearby academic and public libraries, and in graphic slide production.

Cost of the IBM was $4000, which included some software. The HP was a $10,000 purchase. The company will not discuss how much it has spent on additional software packages. The original purchase of the HP was considered a capital expenditure and was made through a formal company procedure. In general the company was supportive of the idea of a micro, and the corporate approval process was quickened by Woodruff's clear idea of what he wanted a micro to do.

Since the HP has become a critical part of the center's operation the company subscribes to Hewlett-Packard's Phone-In-Consultation-Service (PICS). Subscribers can call a toll-free number with any questions regarding HP machines and are guaranteed a response within two hours. Woodruff reports that, in fact, the response time has been short. Cost of the service is about $900 per year.

KITSAP REGIONAL LIBRARY
Bremerton, WA

Type of library: Public
Size of population: 175,000
Type of population: General public
Micros owned: 2 Apple IIs, 3 IBM PCs
Software packages owned: VisiCalc, VisiTrend, VisiPlot, Data Factory, Ontyme, Zardax, dBase II
Software developed in-house: Readability program, dBase II payroll systems
Languages supported: BASIC
Operating systems: DOS 3.3, CP/M

Microcomputer use at the Kitsap Regional Library is largely the result of Michael Schuyler's efforts. He was the main advocate urging the library to acquire a micro, and has become the "computer expert" since Kitsap installed the machines. Since 1981, he has developed a number of software programs, and the machines have become a crucial tool for certain sections of the library.

The Apples are used most extensively by the administration/business office and by the library's art/production department. The art department's Apple, which was acquired in February 1984, is used mainly by the art director for word processing and form generation tasks. This department is also starting to use the Apple to create bibliographies and calendars on disks where they can be easily updated.

The Apple in the administrative office is used for more varied tasks, including such mundane chores as word processing and the maintenance of the entire mailing list for the Washington Library Association. The more creative applications involve the use of customized software, programs that have been tailored by Schuyler for specific uses at Kitsap.

Using dBase II, Schuyler has developed a customized payroll system and "innumerable" VisiCalc templates (software designed to be used in conjunction with other software) for accounting. These include programs for calculating expenditures and revenues, a vacation/sick leave accrual system, a payroll /budget forecasting system, auditing files and other statistical functions. Schuyler has also written other homegrown programs to print purchase orders that are numbered consecutively, mailing lists and an extensive set of text write/read programs to circumvent the bugs in a commercial software data file handler called the Data Factory. In order to help librarians who do not possess a complete understanding of computers to use the micros productively, Schuyler developed some basic programs. He believes that for a library to use micros efficiently it must have at least one staff member at each branch who is well versed with the technology so as to make the transition to micro use as smooth as possible.

Another program developed by Schuyler for Kitsap is the readability program. Using this, a librarian can type in text from a particular book, and have the computer measure the grade level of the material. Schuyler developed the first of these programs for the Apple in 1981, and in winter 1984 converted the program for use on the IBM. The library markets the readability program (the Apple program is priced at $45 and the IBM at $50) to interested libraries. Proceeds from the sales of the programs have been used to acquire additional hardware, including three IBM PCs in spring 1984.

Kitsap has firm plans for using the IBMs. The machines are scheduled to be used as terminals with the Washington Library Network, but will also have other uses such as database searching of local history files and ready reference. Schuyler plans to develop the necessary programs for this application himself, via dBase II.

Although the library uses the micros for a wide range of applications, only a small number of staff members use the machines. Kitsap generally maintains a low-key approach toward staff education on the micros, with only interested staffers given instruction. The library adopted this approach for two reasons—it believes education cannot be forced on people, and the amount of free microcomputer time is very limited. Schuyler, who oversees the training conducted at the library, believes in the dictum that a "personal computer is personal" and that it is not productive to interrupt a computer user to conduct a lesson.

Kitsap has been able to keep the cost of its micro program down because it is eligible for state contract pricing. The library's first Apple system, including software and peripherals, cost approximately $5300. The second Apple system, with less capacity, cost "substantially less," according to Schuyler. The library paid less than $5000 for each of its newly acquired IBMs.

Kitsap has had few mechanical problems with its micros. However, when problems have occurred, repair service has been slow and unreliable, Schuyler reports.

LINCOLN PUBLIC LIBRARY
Springfield, IL

Type of library: Public
Size of population: 100,054
Type of population: General public
Micros owned: 3 Apple II + s, 2 Apple IIes
Software packages owned: Apple Writer, WordStar, VisiCalc, PFS, VisiFile
Software developed in-house: CAI program for database searching
Languages supported: BASIC
Operating systems: Apple DOS

In 1982 Lincoln Library began its micro usage program by acquiring three Apple II + s for its three main departments: administration, reference and public service. Two Apple IIes were acquired in June 1984 for use in a branch library public access program. The extension of the micros into a branch library marks a significant expansion of micro usage since the program began.

When Lincoln initiated the micro program the Apples were pretty much "locked in the administrative office," says James LaRue, assistant library director; no one else on the staff was encouraged to use them. Hoping to spur staff interest, LaRue rewrote the library's computer system manual, altering the instructions so that more programs could be run on the Apples. The result of LaRue's efforts has been a dramatic increase in the use of micros by staff members.

Word processing is the most widely used application for the micros in all three Lincoln departments. Most staff members use Apple Writer for word processing, finding it easier than WordStar, although LaRue does use WordStar for many of his projects. Reports, letters, long-range planning studies and particularly the production and revision of training manuals have been the areas where word processing has proved to be most helpful.

In addition to using the Apples for word processing, the reference department has developed some new databases on the micros. With VisiFile software, the reference department has been using the Apples for serials control. The library has made a listing of all the magazines it subscribes to, the price of the publication, expiration date, vendor acquired from and any routing that is done. LaRue reports that the micro has noticeably cut down on staff time devoted to managing the serials collection. Another database that has been created is the "gift book" database which lists people who have donated funds to the library.

Lincoln's public services department uses VisiCalc to keep track of circulation statistics. When funding becomes available, the library hopes to be able to link its Apples to its CLSI circulation system as a backup. VisiCalc is also used by the library's technical service department for budget analysis.

The most unique aspect of Lincoln's micro program is its dial-up information system for patron use, which was largely designed by LaRue. Using the program, a patron who has a modem can get online access to the library's card catalog via the telephone. The program includes a packet that teaches computer users how to hook up to the system and provides commands; it also prevents unauthorized users from gaining access to other data. Initiated in April 1984, the program has been "fairly well received," LaRue says, noting that "there are a lot of hackers out there." Another telecommunications application for the Apples is accessing local computer bulletin boards. The main purpose is to leave messages about news of the library.

Approximately 18 people on the Lincoln staff use the micros. LaRue provided some initial instruction for individuals requesting it, but for the most part the staff has been self-taught. There was quite a bit of fear among staff members when the micros were first introduced. LaRue says he overcame this fear by demonstrating how the use of the Apple could cut down the time needed to perform the most "odious repetitive task" done by a staff member. "It worked quite well," LaRue says. Although Lincoln has not conducted any formal time/performance surveys, the ability to perform tasks more quickly is the clearest benefit of using the micros. With the increased computer exposure, the staff is now more aware of, and often more competent in, a variety of other computer uses.

Lincoln has spent approximately $4500 on its three main library Apples and related software. The library has had some problems in receiving additional monies to upgrade the system. Lincoln would like to establish a local area network with a hard disk drive, but that program is awaiting funds. At present the three Apples function as stand-alone workstations.

Lincoln was successful, however, in gaining a $5000 LSCA grant for the purchase of two Apple II+s for a public access program for minority children. Established in a branch library in a poor section of the city, the goal of the program is to provide exposure to micros for children who have not had the opportunity to use them either in school or at home. The program was established in June 1984 and 50 children took part in the program in the first month, the maximum number the library could handle. The children are given a 45-minute orientation course on how to use the Apples, and are provided with educational and educational game software. Initial reaction to the free program among parents has been very good; they are "thrilled," LaRue says.

LORAIN PUBLIC LIBRARY
Lorain, OH

Type of library: Public
Size of population: 75,000
Type of population: General public
Micros owned: 7 TRS-80 Model IIIs
Software packages owned: WordStar, VisiCalc, Scripsit, Power Mail,
    plus a variety of educational software and games
Software developed in-house: Label generation program
Languages supported: BASIC, PASCAL
Operating systems: DOS

The use of microcomputers for administrative purposes was a "natural progression" from the Lorain Public Library's computer literacy program, according to Valerie Smith, coordinator of that program. The library launched its public access program in March 1981 and one year later began using the micros, in a limited way, for administrative chores. Lorain has a total of seven TRS-80 micros, five in use at the main library and two at local branches.

The computer literacy program has been very favorably received by the patrons of the Lorain system. The program is open to any library user who is at least eight years of age, completes a computer orientation course and follows the guidelines set forth by Lorain. After taking the 60-minute orientation course, patrons are issued a computer user card. And although anyone younger than eight is not allowed to receive a card, those children can use the micros if they are with an older person.

The guidelines cover almost every aspect of computer use. Micros can only be used during library hours and users must register with the library each time they use the micros. Patrons may book time only once a day, although they are free to use the micros during periods when no bookings are scheduled. Bookings can be made over the phone or in person, no more than seven days in advance. Bookings cannot be transferred and a patron who cannot get to the library must cancel the appointment or he or she will be counted as a no-show. Two no-shows in a month result in a loss of booking privileges for a 30-day period. Users who arrive five minutes late for a booking are subject to loss of their time slot. Patrons may use the micros for games for up to two hours per week in increments of a half hour. Patrons using the micro for educational/informational programs or to practice programming may use the micros for as much as six hours per week in increments of up to three hours. When computer time is not booked the micros are available on a first-come, first-served basis.

Smith reports that approximately 3000 people have taken part in the computer orientation classes, and 70% were under 19 years old. The library has a software inventory of more than 70 programs in both disk and cassette formats. Lorain is also an affiliate of ComputerTown, USA, an association which encourages public access computer programs.

The library has opted to sign service contracts on its machines, contracts that run on the average of 10% to 12% of the purchase price of the machines. However, because of the durability of the machines, Smith says the library is considering having contracts only on equipment with moving parts. "The service contracts have been a godsend for repairing the cassettes," Smith notes. The main reason Lorain chose the TRS-80 machines is that a Radio Shack outlet is located near the library, and the store provides repair service and substantial discounts to the library. "Because we were starting a program for computer beginners we didn't feel we needed to invest in the most sophisticated equipment," Smith explains. The library's TRS-80s, all of which have at least 32K of RAM, and four of which have two disk drives, have served the computer literacy program very well. Lorain started the program to provide computer "self-education to the community," Smith says. The program also serves as good public relations for the library.

Once the micros were set up, the staff began using them for in-house library applications. The library now reserves one disk drive computer, with line printer, for three primary tasks—database management, word processing and mailing list maintenance. Power Mail is used for mailing list purposes while Scripsit is used for word processing functions such as the generation of bibliographies, video program listings and writing library reports. Profile software is used for database management tasks, which have thus far been limited to maintenance of standing book orders or orders in process.

Lorain expects to make only minor additions to its micro operation for administrative purposes. Smith says Lorain anticipates moving to a fully automated system within three to five years, although a specific system has not yet been chosen. Single station micros will serve only in supplementary capacities once such a system is in place. Using micros has made the library staff more comfortable with the idea of computers and technology, and thus is making the switch to an automated system seem more natural.

Funding for the micro program has come from two main sources. The bulk of the money has been provided by the City of Lorain's Community Development Block Grant Program which supplied funds for the purchase of five micros. The library used its own funds to acquire the two other TRS-80s. Smith estimates that Lorain has spent a total of about $16,000 on hardware and software acquisitions.

MAINE STATE LIBRARY
Augusta, ME

Type of library: Public
Size of population: 22,000
Type of population: General public, government officials
Micros owned: 2 TRS-80 Model IIIs, 2 TRS-80 Model IVs
Software packages owned: Scripsit, Superscripsit, Profile III+, VisiCalc, Statpak

Software developed in-house: Programs to expand Profile III+ and
   Scripsit capabilities, and to produce film catalog and indexes
Language supported: BASIC
Operating systems: TRS-DOS 1.3, NEW-DOS 80

Department self-sufficiency was the goal and a "floating" machine
was the method in the early microcomputer program at the Maine State
Library, begun in late 1980. To encourage the use of microcomputers
throughout the library, Donald Wismer, coordinator of automated services, developed a program in which the library's one TRS-80 Model
III was used by different departments in four-hour time blocks. The
machine was housed on a metal table with wheels, and each department was given five diskettes. Another traveling companion of the
micro was a training manual for staff members to use to teach themselves. After approximately one year, library staff members were comfortable with the micros, and three departments—the media services
department, the business office and the TPR (technical processing)
unit—acquired their own machines. This program allowed each department to become well versed with the micro applications most useful
in their particular setting. In addition, because each department operates the micro independently, the program is not dependent on one person for its success.

Scripsit is the software package used most often at Maine State.
It is used for several different applications, including what Wismer believes has been the most helpful use to date, small list management.
With the increased control provided by micros, Maine State has developed approximately 20 small mailing lists. These lists, which include names and addresses of 100 to 2000-member groups, feature such
diverse organizations as Maine radio stations and newspapers to Maine
Online Consortium members. Maine State prints out labels on its daisy
wheel printer, and can merge the mailing lists with text to produce cus-
tom form letters.

Scripsit is also used for catalog and union list production. Both
Maine State's film services and handicapped services departments have
used Scripsit to produce printed book catalogs, rather than card catalogs. Using Scripsit, catalog copy is entered onto hard disks, and the
printer delivers high quality copy that can be arranged in a variety of
ways and typed out in a variety of typefaces. The handicapped services unit, for example, has produced a catalog of large-print books. The

real benefits of the program will come in succeeding years as updating and reprinting of the catalog will be made easier and quicker.

In cooperation with Maine's Special Library Group and Health Science Librarians' Information Cooperative, Maine State has assembled a serials union list for 13 special libraries, again using Scripsit. The catalog contains the holdings of small Maine libraries with interesting collections. The union list is arranged alphabetically by title. A new library is entered by inserting the name in the appropriate spot. Uniprint, a locally developed program, allows holdings for any single library in the list to be typed out. The printout is then sent to the particular library for checking.

VisiCalc is the second most popular software package at Maine State Library. Used primarily by the media services department, VisiCalc is employed to record videotape usage. The library development department uses it for compiling statewide statistics which will later appear in *Libraries of Maine*.

Profile III+ is being used more and more by the library. The business office is using it to track overdue books and to do billing. Profile is also used for serials checkin. Every morning a staff member checks in periodicals and about once a week the file is printed in triplicate and distributed to the circulation and reference departments.

In addition to the commercial software, Maine State has some locally developed programs. The programs have been written either by Wismer or by a library volunteer, and in general the programs are written to expand the capabilities of the commercial packages. For example, the section head of the handicapped services department wanted a way to search for and "tag" all new titles acquired in between printings of the large-print catalog. Using Scripsit, Wismer simply designed a utility program that tagged a new title with an asterisk.

Maine State has had no regrets about the hardware and software it has acquired. However, if the library were getting into the micro field today, it would do things differently. Most important, although the TRS-80 machines have performed admirably, Maine State would equip itself with IBM PCs and, in fact, the next micro purchase will be that of an IBM PC. The main consideration in the change is that the Maine Department of Education has an IBM mainframe, and for the library to be able to develop a network it needs compatible equipment. The TRS-80s will be used for self-contained jobs and will be made available for patron use.

TRS-80s were originally chosen because options were limited when the program was initiated at the end of 1980, and the Radio Shack equipment had the lowest prices. Wismer estimates Maine State has spent $7200 for the micros, $3800 for four printers and about $1000 on software. Maintenance costs have been kept to a minimum. Very little repair has been needed, and Wismer strongly advises against getting service contracts, claiming the expense is not justified.

MANSFIELD-RICHLAND COUNTY PUBLIC LIBRARY
Mansfield, OH

Type of library: Public
Size of population: 131,000
Type of population: General public
Micros owned: 12 TRS-80 Model IIIs
Software packages owned: Approximately 385 different packages for administrative and library functions
Software developed in-house: None
Languages supported: BASIC, COBOL, FORTRAN
Operating systems: TRS-DOS

The emphasis is on public use of microcomputers at the Mansfield-Richland County Public Library. Started in February 1983 by Leslie Lee, director of the library's extension services, Mansfield-Richland's "Love at First Byte" computer literacy program had some 3000 participants through early 1984. Patrons may use the library's micros "for anything they wish," provided they have a county library card and have taken part in the library's computer orientation class. It is the orientation class, coupled with standardized operating rules for public use, that sets the Mansfield-Richland public access program apart from many similar programs at other libraries. Although other libraries have rules for patron use, Mansfield-Richland has been stricter than most in enforcing their rules, and its program has served as a model for patron use programs at other libraries.

Classes are held four to five times per month, with at least one Saturday class each month. Patrons may register for the class by calling the library extension department. Sessions are held at the main library as well as at the system's four branches. Although Lee initially taught the classes, the library has since hired a part-time staff member to conduct the sessions. Each class includes background information on micros, a discussion of basic micro terminology, an explanation of the capabilities of the library's TRS-80s and a demonstration of how a micro actually works. Before a person receives a stamped "computer access card," he or she must be able to run a program. Classes, which generally last one hour, are free.

According to the guidelines established by Lee for both staff and patrons, the number one rule is that no one is allowed to use the micros without first participating in the orientation course. Other guidelines cover pre-booked or walk-in computer users. Patrons may book computer time up to one week in advance by calling either the library switchboard or the particular department where the micro is located when the switchboard is closed. Patrons' requests are all eventually recorded by the switchboard operator on a central booking sheet. Patrons can book no more than six hours of time per week, and only one booking per day per person is allowed. Blocks of time are generally limited to a half hour, although patrons using learning programs or attempting to write their own programs may book up to two hours of time. No-shows may lose booking privileges for 30 days. In the event of a no-show, a walk-in may use the computer. Any free computer time may be used by a walk-in. Patrons that have pre-booked time may also be walk-ins if the micro is free, and such time does not count against the six hour per week limit. Bookings are not transferable.

The library maintains a catalog of available programs at the reference desk in the adult department and at the children's reference desk. A patron chooses the desired program and signs it out on his or her borrower's card. The card remains at the desk while the patron takes the complete envelope with the disk to the computer site. The library provides no technical assistance to the public, and if a problem develops the computer is turned off pending examination by Lee.

Using these guidelines, the computer program has been an unqualified success. The library expected 500 people to use the program in the first year, but had already attracted that many people after the first few months of operation.

Funding for the program came from several sources. The bulk of the initial funding was provided through a $21,000 LSCA grant. The LSCA money, coupled with about $2500 of the library's own funds, was used to acquire six TRS-80 micros, a printer and software packages. An additional $5000 grant from the Richland Foundation was used to help acquire an additional six TRS-80s plus four printers. By early 1984 the grant money had run out, and funds for the project were being taken out of the library's general budget.

With initial hardware purchases covered by the grant money, the library has been allocating its own money only for software purchases and maintenance. Mansfield estimates the library has spent some $3000 on software in the first 14 months of the "Love at First Byte" project. Maintenance costs have been minimal with both hardware and software performing well. Mansfield's acquisition of its first six micros included a provision for a service contract, at 12% of the purchase price, an arrangement which the library determined was not cost efficient. In order to maintain its second group of six computers the library has chosen to use a "loaner" type arrangement with an independent computer repair service. At a cost of $300 per year, the repair service will make minor repairs at $25 per hour, arrange for major repair work and, most important for the library's needs, provide a loaner machine.

The popularity of "Love at First Byte" notwithstanding, Mansfield-Richland's computer program has been largely a one-person show. In addition to her other duties as director of extension services, Lee has overseen the computer project, assuming the role of computer expert. In reality, however, with the exception of a few computer classes, Lee has been mostly self-taught.

As the resident computer pro, Lee has set up programs to allow other library staff members to use the micros for different applications. These applications to date have largely been limited to simple word processing and spreadsheet analysis tasks, although the library has used the micros to monitor some of its accounts with outside companies. Lee believes an important additional benefit of the micros will occur in one or two years when the library implements an automated circulation system. The experience with micros has made both patrons and staff members much more comfortable with computers, and should help to facilitate the eventual change to an automated system.

MORRIS LIBRARY-SPECIAL COLLECTIONS
Southern Illinois University
Carbondale, IL

Type of library: University
Size of population: 2300
Type of population: Faculty, students
Micros owned: 1 TRS-80 Model II, 1 TRS-80 Model 100
Software packages owned: Scripsit, Profile, VisiCalc, KWIX
Software developed in-house: None
Languages supported: BASIC
Operating systems: TRS-DOS

"We use micros so much we don't have time for proper training or experimentation," says David Koch, university archivist and curator of special collections for the Morris Library at Southern Illinois University at Carbondale, in describing Carbondale's micro program. The two TRS-80s at the Morris Library are in use an estimated nine hours a day and are used by all members of the library staff as well as by student assistants.

The ability of student workers to use the micros is one of the most important reasons for a library to have a machine, Koch maintains. When budget cuts eliminated several staff members from the library work force, the micros allowed student assistants to take over some routine library chores. For example, students help sort different types of data into different categories, and the micro ensures that the correct information is entered in the proper place (e.g., that data are entered in the correct chronological or alphabetical order). In addition, micros allow one to "demand perfection" from student aids, Koch reports. "Before we began using micros for word processing, if a student came close to writing a letter without any errors we let it pass, but now we want everything letter perfect."

The Morris Library uses three basic software programs—Scripsit (for word processing), VisiCalc (for statistical manipulation) and Profile (for database management). Although the library's first exposure to micros was word processing, Morris has since developed more creative database applications using Profile packages. The library has created small databases that catalog different mailing lists, such as

Friends of Library and donors. Profile is also used to monitor the library's inventory, allowing the library staff to quickly update any changes in its supplies and materials. Profile is particularly good for creating databases of small collections. Morris has placed all university archives and all university publications on disks. Morris plans to move to hard disk capability during the 1984–1985 academic year.

The heavy, continuous use of the library's original TRS-80 Model II led the library to acquire a Model 100 in the 1983–1984 school year to help ease the load of the Model II. The Model 100 is tied to the Model II, and Morris downloads all its data into the larger machine. These are not integrated with any other micros, either in other sections of the library or with other university departments. "We wanted to avoid having anything to do with the university mainframe," Koch explains, noting that the Morris collection and the administration office have separate needs. Koch says that "down the line" the Morris collection and the other sections of the library may standardize their systems, but at present he is satisfied with his stand-alone operation.

The TRS-80s have exceeded Koch's expectations, and have been very reliable. The decision to acquire the TRS-80 Model II was made in part because, at the time of the purchase in 1981, it was the biggest machine available. More important, however, was the ability of Radio Shack to provide service for the machine. Radio Shack has also provided some instruction. The bulk of micro training, however, is done by the library itself. A word processing specialist oversees the use of the micros and gives some instruction, while other instruction is provided through software tutorials.

Without staff cuts and increased demands on the time of remaining staff members, Koch believes the cost of the micro program, about $7500 for the two machines and software, has been a bargain.

MUDD LEARNING CENTER
Oberlin College
Oberlin, OH

Type of library: University
Size of population: 3000

Type of population: Faculty, students
Micros owned: 4 Osbornes, 1 Intel MDS
Software packages owned: WordStar, SuperCalc, dBase II
Software developed in-house: Circulation backup
Languages supported: BASIC, PL M 80
Operating systems: ISIS, CP/M

Microcomputers are used for two distinct purposes at the Mudd Learning Center on the Oberlin College Campus. Since 1977 the library has used an Intel MDS micro as a backup for its mainframe circulation system, and has been using Osborne micros since 1983 to assist with library administrative functions. The decision to use Osborne micros was based largely on the fact that the Oberlin Computer Center had negotiated a distribution agreement with the Osborne Computer Corp., enabling the computer center to supply Osbornes to the Oberlin community at wholesale prices. The agreement also made Oberlin an authorized repair facility. Even though Osborne Computer Corp. has since filed bankruptcy the college continues to have an agreement with the company, although the terms have changed.

Oberlin uses the four Osbornes primarily for word processing and database management applications. WordStar is used to perform standard word processing tasks—letter writing, development of how-to guides for student assistants and creation of patron guides. The Osbornes are also used in a more unique moneymaking project. The library compiles updates of the Rules of Cataloging issued by the Library of Congress, prints the rules out on the Osbornes (the library owns Okidata 84 and Diablo 630 printers) and sells the reports on a quarterly basis to interested institutions.

dBase II software is used by Oberlin mainly for cataloging smaller collections that otherwise would be too expensive to catalog. Such collections usually contain fewer than 100 items, and are cataloged using keywords, such as the author's name and title of the materials. An example of one such catalog is the college's music collection.

Oberlin has adopted a go-slow approach to the micros, implementing different applications only when it is sure the library has the necessary equipment to accomplish a given task. One source of frustration has been the problems Oberlin has had trying to establish a library network system. Oberlin wants to purchase a Winchester disk and web networking software to enable a series of Osbornes, including machines located at college branch libraries, to access the hard disk simultaneously. However, Osborne's network system is limited to a distance of only 50 feet, far too short for its needs. Experts in the college's electronics department have been studying the problem and hope to have a solution soon.

The library's operating budget includes a line for computer equipment and software which Katherine Frohmberg, systems librarian in charge of the college's micro operation, admits the library has exceeded. The micro allocation, however, is not extensive. The college has purchased only a few software packages, and hardware costs have been kept to approximately $5000 because of the discounts the college received on the Osbornes.

Frohmberg, who teaches a five-hour computer course every semester, teaches the staff how to use the micros. Reaction to the machines has been mixed among Oberlin staff members. Frohmberg has overcome the most serious resistance by assigning micro projects that have a direct impact on the staff member's job. As systems librarian, Frohmberg is in charge of increasing the automation of the library and has found that using micros is a good way to introduce the staff to new technologies.

Frohmberg is also responsible for the automated circulation system which Oberlin has been using since 1977 and which has as a key component an Intel MDS micro. The circulation system features the Xerox Sigma 9 mainframe which uses the CP/M operating system, has 128K memory and uses six disk drives of 80 megabyte capacity each. The Intel MDS uses a 64K byte memory core, ISIS II operating system and two floppy diskettes of one-half megabyte capacity each for logging transactions when the Sigma is down.

The Intel plays a significant role in the operation of the system. It performs a number of tasks including the following: identifies terminal and branch locations so an operator need not enter branch locations; automatically assigns the loan period for the majority of borrower categories; formats transactions to the Sigma by computing check digits and barcode labels; prompts system operators; acts as a multiplexer by managing six terminals on one line; allows logging of transactions when the Sigma is not available; and times various functions for statistical purposes.

Although the micro can perform many different routine circulation functions, such as allocating books to reserve, locking out delinquent patrons and searching for books by author and/or title, its most important function is circulation backup.

When it is in an offline mode the micro times every transaction it sends to the Sigma mainframe. If it receives no response after three minutes, the micro severs communication with the Sigma and logs the transaction on the floppy diskettes. Until the operator tries to bring the system online, the micro will log transactions on the diskettes, a function that is valuable when the Sigma crashes and when the response is very slow. When the Sigma does become available for use, transactions are unwound to the online database.

Oberlin acknowledges that, in terms of technology, its circulation system is old. Nonetheless, the system, including the Intel MDS, has performed well for the school. It is likely the entire system will be replaced when the college mainframe is replaced.

NATIONAL AGRICULTURAL LIBRARY
Beltsville, MD

Type of library: Research
Size of population: Approximately 7000
Tyep of population: U.S. Department of Agriculture professionals
Micros owned: 5 IBM PCs, 2 Compaqs, 1 Apple II, 1 Lanier, 1 Alpha
     Micro
Software packages owned: VisiCalc, WordStar, dBase II
Software developed in-house: None
Languages supported: BASIC, PASCAL, Micro-Assembler
Operating systems: MS, PC DOS, CP/M 86

The U.S. Department of Agriculture National Agricultural Library (NAL) has been using micros for routine business chores such as spreadsheet analysis, word processing and general ledger work since 1978. While these applications have been useful, it is some newer applications, as well as some plans for the immediate future, that hold the most excitement for Philip Turner, chief of the information systems division at the library. NAL's plans include the development of an interactive videodisc, completion of a project about animals called the FARAD (Food, Animal, Residue, Avoidance Database) project and the in-house development of a data entry software program. The library's most recent application has been the development of an interlibrary loan program.

The basis of the interlibrary loan system, launched in June 1984, is NAL's Apple which is used in conjunction with OCLC's ILL (interlibrary loan) microcomputer enhancer program. The micro enhancer program provides telecommunications capabilities and allows NAL to interface with other OCLC clients by making the Apple compatible with other hardware. The interlibrary loan program is run by librarians in NAL's lending and utilization branch. NAL had some early problems getting the Apple to work properly with the OCLC enhancer software, but Turner was able to resolve the problem using a Quadrom Corp. Quadlink board. The interlibrary loan program was "very successful" in its first month of operation, Turner says.

NAL's interactive videodisc program is being developed by an outside firm. When completed, the videodisc will serve as an interactive training program on information retrieval. Specifically, the videodisc will operate in conjunction with an IBM PC to train NAL and USDA employees to use NAL's AGRICOLA database.

Two cooperative programs are also under development at NAL involving the use of micros. One program involves the development of a data entry program by the NAL staff. NAL hopes to increase the amount of agricultural literature available in its AGRICOLA database through cooperative agreements with state land grant colleges. Under the program, land grant schools that have access to an IBM PC would be given NAL-provided software to record and enter news items about agriculture in machine-readable format. The data would then be returned electronically to NAL and added to the AGRICOLA database. Development of the NAL data entry package is crucial to the success of the project, for it is NAL's contention that it is critical to enter the new data correctly the first time. Turner warns that there is "nothing worse than trying to correct incorrectly entered data."

A second cooperative program involves NAL and different state agricultural agencies in the creation of FARAD. Using an IBM PC and dBase II software, FARAD will be used to maintain pharmacokinetic data—or information on how residue ingested by animals interacts with an animal's system. This type of data is necessary, for example, to determine if it would be safe to slaughter an animal that had eaten food containing certain chemicals. As new pharmacokinetic information is added to FARAD, NAL will foward the materials to six different locations. This is not a true networking system in that the information is not sent electronically. Rather, the new materials are sent on floppy disks through the mail. Funding for the project is being supplied by different state agencies, with NAL contributing its resources.

The Food Nutrition Center, recently transferred to the USDA, also uses micros. The Center uses an IBM PC and an Apple in classes it conducts for nutrition and diet teachers. Programs are used as educational tools to demonstrate the benefits of certain foods and diets.

NAL's current micro projects have developed through experience. The library's first micro was an Alpha Micro, acquired in 1978. It was originally intended to be used to access online databases, retrieve citations and process them locally. However, the hardware proved to be inadequate for these needs and the software supplied never lived up to expectations. Subsequently, the manufacturer upgraded the operating system, but in doing so the software packages were made totally incompatible with the new system. Through this experience NAL learned a number of lessons: the importance of software, the need to choose hardware based on the library's requirements and the need for a standardized micro system.

With this background, the library purchased IBM PCs and PC-compatible Compaqs in 1982. Reasons for choosing the IBM included its easy-to-use keyboard, ease of expandability and the high maintenance and repair reputation of IBM. The IBMs and the Compaqs now form the basis of NAL's micro system. The Apple is limited to use in the interlibrary loan program and does not interact with other library programs. In addition, the library owns some Lanier microcomputer word processing systems. The Lanier is used heavily for such tasks as correspondence and mailing lists, but for little else.

Turner estimates that NAL has spent approximately $35,000 on its most recent hardware purchases—five IBM PCs, two Compaqs and an Apple II. Acquisitions are made on Turner's recommendations and after approval by the library director. Software expenditures have totaled approximately $8000. As chief of the information systems division, Turner is responsible for the maintenance and repair of the micros. He reports that all the hardware has performed very well, with the most serious problem being a burned-out hard disk. To facilitate repairs NAL has a service contract with a local, independent repair company.

NATIONAL BUREAU OF STANDARDS LIBRARY
Washington, DC

Type of library: Research
Size of population: 3000
Type of population: Scientists, engineers
Micros owned: 3 Apple II+s, 1 Seequa Chameleon, 1 Kaypro II, 1 Epson HX-20
Software packages owned: VisiCalc, Perfect Writer, User Link, others
Software developed in-house: Classification and serial checkin packages
Languages supported: BASIC, PASCAL, MUMPS
Operating systems: DOS 3.3, MS DOS, CP/M

Microcomputers perform only limited functions at the National Bureau of Standards Library (NBSL) since many of the functions that micros can perform, particularly in circulation, have been taken over by a newly installed integrated library system. The new system has also absorbed the energies of the staff which would otherwise have been devoted to the development of micro applications.

NBSL first acquired micros—the three Apples—to use for computer-assisted instruction of hearing-impaired library technicians. The specially developed software in the program was compatible only with Apples. However, NBSL found it had very little use for this particular application; now the Apples are used for budgeting, word processing and public relations activities.

The public relations application is somewhat unique. The library modified a commercial program which intersperses color graphics and short messages on a CRT to advertise various library programs and activities such as Library Week. The screen was placed near the library entrance to attract attention, and the programs were developed along the lines of "point of sale" promotions in a bid to interest patrons. This practice met with only mild response, but is still used on occasion.

Another unique application of the micros is a study project designed to develop performance standards. The project consisted of checking staff members' work throughout the course of the day. Since the person in charge of the project checked the work at different times on different days, a clock (time-keeping) program was developed to sound an alarm at the appropriate time.

The Epson, Kaypro and Seequa Chameleon micros were all acquired with money that was budgeted to upgrade NBSL's minicomputer operation. The library determined that the most efficient way to improve its minicomputer programs was through the acquisition of micros; it is too time-consuming to train staff to use a mini, but micros can be used to supplement the work of the minis. Because different people using the terminals would have different needs, NBSL did not worry about standardizing the micro purchases. All the different micros are, however, able to communicate with one another. The Kaypro, used primarily by the reference department, is used for word processing and statistical management tasks, using Perfect Writer software. The Seequa Chameleon micro, a manager's workstation, is used for word processing, communications and spreadsheet functions. The Epson was obtained in early 1984 to be used with User Link program, a communications program to access databases. By spring 1984, however, the library "hadn't gotten very far with the program," according to Marvin Brown, chief of resources development. He blamed the slow progress on a lack of time.

Although the micros have been used for limited purposes at NBSL, the library has been generally pleased with the performance of the machines. Budget applications have been of the greatest benefit to NBSL and the library is in the process of developing spreadsheet templates for further library statistics compilation. In addition, the library has ordered an IBM PC which will be used solely for budget programs.

NBSL has spent slightly more than $10,000 on micro hardware and approximately $1000 on software. An important consideration in acquiring the Kaypro and Epson micros was that the purchase price included software. Brown says obtaining funding for the micros can be a complicated procedure, but nothing too much out of the ordinary from typical bureaucratic process. Training of staff members on the machines is a "hit or miss" proposition, Brown says, with no one person actually in charge of micro education. Brown, in his capacity as chief of resources development, is nominally in charge of the overall micro program. He has acquired most of the machines and oversees what maintenance is done on them. To date none of the micros has presented Brown with a major problem.

NATIONAL LIBRARY OF CANADA
Public Services Branch
Ottawa, ONT

Type of library: Reference, research
Size of population: NA
Type of population: Researchers, other Canadian libraries
Micros owned: 6 IBM PCs, 2 Apple II+s
Software packages owned: WordStar, Lotus 1-2-3, Inmagic, Gutenberg
Software developed in-house: Index to videodisc project
Languages supported: BASIC, PASCAL (Apple)
Operating systems: DOS

The Public Services Branch is one of four branches of the National Library of Canada that has jumped on the microcomputer bandwagon. In April 1984 the branch bought six IBMs and one Apple II+ to join the Apple II+ it had acquired several years earlier. The newly acquired machines are being used by the branch in several different applications, while the original Apple II+ is continuing to be used to index the contents of the library's videodisc project.

The original Apple II+ is linked to a DiscoVision Associates videodisc player in a project designed to demonstrate the storage and retrieval capabilities of a combined micro/videodisc system. The Apple stores and retrieves the index to more than 1200 frames of text stored on the videodisc. The index is written in both English and French. The software for the project was written by the branch's own in-house programmer. The Apple is also used with the VisiCalc software for some spreadsheet functions.

The new Apple II+ was bought to operate Gutenberg software in an experimental project. Started in summer 1984, the experiment is designed to determine the feasibility of using micros to develop a multilingual bibliography comprising 27 different languages.

Three of the IBM PCs are being used primarily as part of the National Library of Canada's interlibrary loan program. Using PC Net software, the three machines are linked to the library's Office of Network Development, in a pilot project of an automated interlibrary loan (ILL) workstation. The pilot project, which was nearing completion when this book went to press, has four main objectives:

1. To assess the need for, and effectiveness of, the ILL system;
2. To assess how user-friendly the system is;

3. To conduct a user-impact assessment; and
4. To identify other features which could be incorporated.

The features that can be supported are: facilitating message preparation with attractively displayed forms; verifying the accuracy and completeness of entered information; keeping track of the status of all outstanding loan transactions; allowing message preparation one at a time or in batches; and providing a user-friendly menu-driven system with extensive help facilities as well as shortcuts for more experienced users.

A fourth IBM is being used with Lotus 1-2-3 to develop more complete library performance statistics. The branch would like to improve its methods of measuring the activity conducted by the library. The micro will help by allowing the library to create special calculations for studying the data collected and to generate more meaningful graphs. The branch's documentation center is using Inmagic software for word processing functions on another IBM. The micro is being used to create an index, with multi-access points, to the center's holdings. A sixth IBM will be used by the library's reference desk. Although no specific applications had been developed by summer 1984, the library anticipates using Inmagic software to enhance its reference files.

Despite the fact that the staff was eager to obtain the machines, the implementation of different applications has occurred more slowly than the branch had anticipated. "It has taken longer for the staff to become comfortable with the machines than we thought," Carol Lunau, senior adviser and systems analyst, says. Although the implementation process has been slow the demand for micros is still so great the branch may acquire three or four more in 1985.

The Public Services Branch, as well as other National Library branches, has the freedom, and the responsibility, to acquire whatever hardware and software programs it wants. Lunau is in charge of coordinating the Public Services Branch's micro activities, including acquisitions. The approach the branch has adopted is to let the available software determine what hardware to acquire. The library determines what software it needs through discussions with the library's "line managers" (department heads). It was because of this approach that the second Apple II+ in particular was acquired, since the Apple can operate the Gutenberg software the library needs for its multilingual experiment. The decision to acquire the IBMs was also based on the available software as well as the reliability of operation the IBM name implies.

System compatibility was not a high priority for either the Public

Services Branch or the National Library when considering what hardware to acquire. First, the library had decided that its early applications would be mostly stand-alone functions, and second, the library was more interested in getting the micro program underway than in system compatibility. Indeed, throughout the National Library system there are a number of different micros, including Apples, IBMs, Northern Telecoms, Commodores and an NCR. Nonetheless, as the program matures, the National Library is considering making the IBM the standard micro. The library has plans to establish a local area network (LAN) with the first benefit being peripheral sharing (sharing of peripheral pieces of hardware). It is doubtful, however, that the National Library will move toward a completely centralized micro program.

In addition to examining the possibility of establishing a LAN, the National Library has taken other steps toward coordinating the micro efforts of its different branches. All acquisitions, both of hardware and software, must be approved by a central micro policy committee. The National Library also maintains an inventory list of all its hardware and software holdings. Information about the software, including evaluations of the materials, is shared among the different branches. The inventory list is also used to avoid buying duplicates of software; however, if the branches that want the software are far apart they are free to acquire duplicate packages. These central procedures notwithstanding, each branch of the National Library is largely responsible for determining its own micro needs, including the training of the staff and the maintenance of the hardware.

The commitment to micros is firm at the National Library of Canada. The library estimates it has spent Can$200,000 on hardware and software and expects to make additional purchases in the future.

NORTH-PULASKI BRANCH LIBRARY
The Chicago Public Library
Chicago, IL

Type of library: Public
Size of population: 83,289
Type of population: General public

Micros owned: 1 Apple II+
Software packages owned: More than 2000 programs—from games to
    programming packages
Software developed in-house: None
Languages supported: Applesoft, Apple Integer
Operating systems: DOS 3.3

The personal computer center at Chicago's North-Pulaski Library
was started in late 1981 as a test vehicle to examine the possibility of
establishing other centers in other Chicago locations. The brainchild
of Patrick Dewey, then branch librarian at North-Pulaski, the computer
center provides public access to microcomputers. It features an Apple
II+ microcomputer with two disk drives, monochromatic monitor,
Hayes modem, Epson MX–70 printer and language card. Price of the
initial purchase for all the hardware mentioned was $4370, and the
funds were provided by a grant from the Friends of the Library.

The Apple was chosen because the staff had had experience with
the machine, and there was a significant amount of software available. The Apple also had a good reputation for operating reliability, and,
in fact, the machine has rarely broken down. Although North-Pulaski
still carries a service contract for the machine, it decided that the more
expensive on-site contract it originally obtained wasn't needed.

The public access program is open to patrons of all ages. North-
Pulaski has been successful in attracting a significant number of adults
to the center, and approximately 40% of the program's participants are
over the age of 21. The library attributes its ability to attract adults to
both its marketing efforts and its extensive software collection. North-
Pulaski's marketing efforts include coverage of the program in the local
press as well as the creation of a library newsletter, *Public Computing*.

The library's extensive software holdings have been pruned somewhat. North-Pulaski found it had to abandon its arcade games because
of management problems. Children were booking the computer for
weeks at a time to play arcade games, preventing other patrons from
having time at the computer. Game playing days were instituted, but
this failed to solve the problem, since more children signed up for the
time slots than the library had available.

North-Pulaski's software inventory still boasts over 2000 programs
on some 200 disks. The collection was built in large part from donations; the library has a software budget of only $650 per year. Early
statistics showed that some 35% of all persons using the center were

interested in educational software programs such as Typing Tutor. About half of the patrons were interested in using educational games.

In addition to the arcade game experience, another misstep in developing the center was an attempt by the library staff to teach a "crash course" on the operation of the Apple. North-Pulaski found that the staff time involved in the program was too great to justify the return. The idea behind the course was to get patrons familiar with the Apple. However, the library discovered that the most effective way to do this is to offer a 10-minute orientation course during which a staff member quickly runs a patron through the basic operation of the Apple. The library has also created a "User's Guide" handbook which lists rules of the program, hours and available software. In addition, North-Pulaski has a number of tutorial software programs on hand for patrons to use, such as Apple Presents Apple.

Patrons are advised to book computer time (one hour at a time) in advance. Patrons are not limited to a certain hour per week, but only one appointment at a time can be made. The library estimates that an average of 200 patrons per month participate in the program.

Although the micro is used by patrons much of the working day, North-Pulaski staff members do use the Apple on occasion. Using Data Factory software, the library has created a subject guide wall chart of some 550 different subject headings with corresponding Dewey and Library of Congress classification numbers. North-Pulaski estimates that this program saves between one-half to one-third of the time the staff previously spent on reference work, and serves as a backup to its COM catalog. The library has also developed an inventory for its software collection as well as a delinquent list file (list of patrons with overdues).

Marvin Garber, the assistant librarian who oversees the computer center, acknowledges that he would like to have greater access to the Apple for his own use, but says he is a victim of the center's success. Any time funds become available for the purchase of new machines, the money is allocated for the acquisition of micros for other Chicago branch libraries. And, although more micros are being acquired, there are no immediate plans for the Chicago library system to network the different micros.

The Apple also plays an important role in North-Pulaski's electronic bulletin board. The bulletin board generates 1000 calls a month. The system currently in use at North-Pulaski is the People's Message System (PMS). (The library originally used the Apple Bulletin Board

System, but discontinued the program, mainly because of system break-downs and maintenance problems.)

The PMS at North-Pulaski allows patrons to read and leave messages, read feature material and download public domain computer programs. Any patron who owns a modem can connect with the library and participate in the bulletin board program. Because the bulletin board is a public access program, passwords are assigned only for convenience. When a patron signs on, the micro enters the proper name, address and other log-on information. After logging on, the patron can choose a variety of options, including featured articles or message files.

The downloading of public domain software was added in January 1984. Anyone calling the library can access the available programs, provided they have a computer, a modem and a telecommunications or terminal software package, such as ASCII Express. Available bulletin board programs appear under the PROG label at North-Pulaski, and downloading instructions are also available online.

A certain amount of maintenance is needed to keep the bulletin board running smoothly, such as the clearing of the log file and the system each day. The addition of new articles and features also requires some time. The log file has served a number of useful purposes for the North-Pulaski bulletin board, particularly the maintenance of statistics. In December 1983, statistics showed that for 92 consecutive callers the average call was 15 minutes long. Only 12 callers stayed online for less than five minutes.

North-Pulaski estimates that it takes about 10 minutes to one hour each morning to take the PMS system down. In addition to reading the log file, this involves running off messages and responding to them. At night, inserting the diskettes to prepare it for running takes about five minutes. The library advises that the most important part of maintaining a good system is backing up the diskettes (making duplicates). The North-Pulaski bulletin board is backed up six times each week and there are six sets of backup diskettes plus a master copy.

To avoid micro system failure, North-Pulaski recommends libraries follow six steps: install a fan; clean the computer regularly; back up diskettes frequently and replace working diskettes every three months; install a surge protector, if necessary; use a unique password system; and make sure to plug the telephone line back in after disconnecting for maintenance. Although North-Pulaski has had a few problems with crank calls, it has instituted some preventive methods. The library has installed an obscenity filter which automatically checks each message against an operator-defined file of undesirable words. If the message contains one, it is refused. North-Pulaski suggests a call to the local police station if threatening messages come in.

NOVO LABORATORIES LIBRARY
Wilton, CT

Type of library: Corporate
Size of population: 75
Type of population: Professional
Micros owned: 1 Apple II
Software packages owned: Apple Writer, WordStar, dBase II, VisiCalc, VisiDex
Software developed in-house: dBase II programs
Languages supported: Applesoft, Apple Integer, MBASIC, GBASIC, PASCAL
Operating systems: DOS, CP/M

Like the corporate library itself, Novo Laboratories' microcomputer operation is compact and efficient. The microcomputer, an Apple II with 96K memory, is used only by Novo's two-person library staff, which is under the direction of Jim Fleagle. Fleagle, who also oversees the use of the micro, had no previous experience with the machines when the library prepared to buy its first micro in 1981. His only exposure had been at a local library group workshop where he decided micros could be a useful addition to Novo's library. To justify the acquisition, Fleagle explained to his superiors that the micro was necessary for online searching. The volume of online searching was steadily increasing at the library, but on such occasions it was necessary for Fleagle to borrow a terminal from another department. Fleagle's argument was convincing, and the funds for the purchase were approved.

Although online searching is still the most widely used application, the Apple is also used in a number of different ways with Novo's journal collection. Using VisiDex software, Novo has implemented a journal circulation system for more than 300 titles. The micro manages the company's circulation lists and records a listing of every publication to which Novo subscribes. To route the journals, Fleagle simply punches in each journal's code, and a mailing list label is produced. The journals are then "remailed" to the appropriate personnel.

dBase II software is used to maintain Novo's serials catalog. The Apple maintains information on all the serials the library has, and the status of each, whether the particular item is bound, in microfiche form or in storage. The serial holdings can also be printed out by category; if a staff member wants to know what computer magazines the library owns, for example, the Apple can produce that list.

Another application for the Apple has been the creation of two small databases. One is an index to all Novo lab reports. A second database, known as the computerized intelligence file, provides an index to all the documents in the corporate files pertaining to Novo competitors. The Apple is also used for run-of-the mill word processing functions and Fleagle is working on some programs in the accounting area. Specifically, he is working on programs that break out different kinds of searches that are conducted, so that each department can be billed for the searches they do.

Although Fleagle has developed some of his own programs, he feels that in general the commercially available packages provide a good basis for getting a micro program going. The availability of software was a key factor in his decision to acquire the Apple in 1981. At that time, Fleagle notes, the Apple offered the greatest abundance of quality software. If he were starting over again today, Fleagle said he would choose the IBM PC, "only because that seems to be the way the software is going." Other factors that influenced his choice of the Apple were the solid reputation of the company ("We knew Apple was going to be around for awhile.") and the availability of service. In the service end Fleagle notes that he does not have a service contract "and never will." He estimates that in the three years Novo has had the Apple he has spent about $50 on repairs.

Fleagle estimates that he has spent a total of nearly $10,000 on the micro, with the price including a hard disk drive and a NEC spinwriter 7700 printer. The letter quality printer has never given Fleagle any trouble and has been an invaluable asset. Fleagle's micro has done more than just improve the productivity of the library, it has also broken down a lot of stereotypes of the corporate library, Fleagle believes. "Lots of employees thought of us as a public library in a corporate setting; now they are starting to realize we can offer more service than just a place to store materials," he says.

PLAINFIELD PUBLIC LIBRARY
Plainfield, NJ

Type of library: Public
Size of population: 45,600
Type of population: General public
Micros owned: 2 TRS-80 Model IIIs, 5 TRS-80 Model IIs, 1 TRS-80 Model 16B
Software packages owned: Scripsit, Profile+, VisiCalc, Multiplan, dBase II
Software developed in-house: Film booking and financial information system packages
Languages supported: BASIC, COBOL, FORTRAN, C
Operating systems: TRS-DOS, CP/M 2.2, DOS plus II, XENIX

Microcomputers "pay for themselves" at the Plainfield Public Library. According to Thomas Ballard, library director, "the microcomputer is of enormous benefit to libraries because we have so many paperwork functions. We file, we write, we make lists, etc. All of these functions have been very labor-intensive and expensive. By providing better tools, we can reduce staff. From 26 full-time persons in 1981, we have reduced this to 19."

Thomas Ballard was the main force behind Plainfield's entry into the micro field. The owner of a micro himself, Ballard was sure that the machines could reduce the library's paperwork, and convinced the Friends of the Plainfield Library Association to acquire a TRS-80. At the same time Plainfield adopted a strategy of reducing staff levels at its own discretion, before the fiscal situation absolutely required it to do so.

The savings realized from this action were then used to purchase additional micros, Ballard said, "to improve the productivity in paperwork functions of the remaining personnel" Plainfield purchased $50,000 worth of hardware and $7000 to $8000 in software. The system features five TRS-80s with 64K memory, two with 128K memory and a Model 16B with 512K memory, which supports five terminals.

Micros were first used by Plainfield to perform word processing tasks such as letter writing, development of board agendas, treasurer's reports and other monthly tasks. After the staff became more familiar with the micros, more complex functions, such as simple database management, were developed. This allowed the library to monitor its various lists.

The library's technical service department is the most automated section of the library, using micros to process book orders and to compile statistics. The micros are also used to generate mailing lists, which has resulted in the retirement of Plainfield's old label machine. Ballard has also written a management information program in BASIC which is used to monitor the library's finances. The program compares each library account with the prior year and makes expenditure projections for the coming year. Ballard's program is also used to sort out the library's endowment fund. It allows the library's bookkeeper to quickly and correctly allocate funds to the proper programs after receiving the money in one lump sum from the bank.

In addition to speeding completion of routine administrative functions, the micros at Plainfield are used to do things the library previously could not do. For example, the library recently acquired nearly 100 years' worth of architectural drawings from the city (drawings which were required before building permits were issued). These drawings have been cataloged along several different reference points, such as original architect and street address, for ease of access. Furthermore, using dBase II, Plainfield created an associate file which includes the purchase price of each house, plus any available pictures.

The most recent application for the micros has been in Plainfield's circulation department. Ballard believes the size of the collection does not justify the expense of an automated circulation system, or the additional costs of maintenance contracts. But there are elements of automation that Ballard likes, and he has adapted some of these into a micro system. Using Radio Shack's Profile + system, Ballard created a program that tracks delinquent patrons. By typing the first two letters of the last name of a patron, a librarian can determine if a borrower has any fines outstanding. If so, the book loan is refused until the fines are paid. The circulation system is also being used to print overdue notices.

Plainfield conducts no formal computer training classes for its staff. When a staff member indicates an interest in micros, Ballard provides him or her with a manual and a machine with which to experiment. To facilitate the training of interested staff Plainfield will soon be acquiring modems so that "traveling terminals" can be taken home for staff use. In addition, when a micro becomes obsolete it may be used for training purposes. Any obsolete micros will also be made available for patron use. To date, Plainfield provides no public access machines.

Maintenance of Plainfield's micros is done as needed. Ballard is vehemently opposed to maintenance contracts believing that the costs are "ridiculously high." "If we needed maintenance contracts to maintain the micros I never would have started the program," he asserts, adding that reliability is a distinct advantage micros have over minicomputers. Ballard estimates that in the three years Plainfield has been using micros the library has spent no more than $400 on repairs. When a repair is needed the micro is brought to one of the three computer centers within 10 miles of the library.

Ballard also has some advice for librarians who are looking at micros. For one thing, he cautions, "micros only really save money when there are no bottlenecks and no waiting [to use the machines]." Further, he notes that there are three elements to consider when moving into the micro field–"hardware, software and realizing what to do with the first two. The last takes time. Staff must have access to the equipment before this process even begins. We've been at it for nearly three years and our greatest benefits are yet to come."

POINT PLEASANT HIGH SCHOOL LIBRARY
Point Pleasant, WV

Type of library: Senior high school
Size of population: 675
Type of population: Students and faculty
Micros owned: 1 TRS-80 Model III
Software packages owned: None
Software developed in-house: Automated Library System
Languages supported: BASIC
Operating systems: TRS-DOS, DOS, DOSPLUS

In many respects Point Pleasant High School has set the standard for the efficient use of microcomputers by small-to-medium sized high schools. Under the direction of head librarian Judy Graham, Point Pleasant has developed the Automated Library System (ALS), a completely integrated library reference, circulation and accounting system, which performs some 30 different library functions.

ALS enables library users to search an electronic catalog for titles, authors and subjects. It also performs a number of bookkeeping and administrative functions for the library staff such as assessing daily fines on overdue books, listing the status of books and borrowers, printing due and overdue notices and listing them according to homeroom, maintaining accounts on outstanding fines, printing shelf lists, tallying the volumes that have been added to the collection during a specific time period, determining which volumes have been added to the noncirculating list and preparing statistics for state and national library reports.

ALS developed through the efforts of three people: Judy Graham, M. William Dunklau, a computer consultant from Dallas who developed the Simu-School project and James Hopson, a student at Point Pleasant at the time. With no background in micros, Graham discussed her basic idea for the school system with Dunklau. She wanted a user-friendly, integrated system that could perform various routine library functions. Dunklau developed the framework for ALS, including the programming, sorting and merging of the system, while Hopson did much of the actual implementation at Point Pleasant.

Using ALS, the library maintains circulation by entering the student number and book accession number (books are given sequential numbers as they are acquired) into the microcomputer at checkout time. The computer provides student name, homeroom and book title. Before a book is cleared, the student number will allow the librarian to see if the student has any overdue books or outstanding fines. If such is the case the checkout is blocked until all fines are paid. If a student has no fines, the micro will verify the student number, and then ask for the book's accession number to use as a control number. When the accession number is entered the checkout procedure is complete. To check in materials, the accession number is entered into the computer and the book is automatically removed from the circulation files. As an integral part of the circulation process, ALS records all outstanding fines and maintains current balances.

ALS also allowed Point Pleasant to create an electronic card catalog that contains approximately 12,000 titles. The catalog lists title, author, accession number, copyright date, publisher, subjects and current borrower information. To create the electronic catalog, which took some four months, Graham entered the desired information on five one-quarter-inch floppy disks, each of which holds data on 333 volumes. A total of 2.5 million characters were typed onto the floppy disks.

When using the catalog a student indicates which type of search is desired (author, title, etc.) by pressing the appropriate key. After the choice has been made, the screen displays the author, title, call number and accession number, status of the book and all subject headings. By using ALS, patrons are almost immediately able to determine if a book is in the library or has been checked out. If a book is out the due date and the name of the borrower are automatically provided.

Through a "print reports" function ALS enables the Point Pleasant library to do a number of other tasks. Bibliographies can be prepared for faculty and students in seconds, by subject, title and author. Statistics are also more easily compiled. Due or overdue notices are printed out and sent to the homeroom or the individual student. These notices can later be retrieved electronically, if needed. Daily, monthly and yearly circulation statistics by classifications are prepared by the computer and circulation analysis is available by subject, author, call number and accession number. The number of times each book has been circulated is recorded and can be obtained by searching under any of the classifications mentioned above. All noncirculated volumes can be listed and eliminated from the collection, while new volumes added to the collection can be printed and distributed to students and faculty members. A complete inventory can be printed by accession number or call number.

In addition, ALS allows new books and names of new students to be easily added to the system. An inquiry selection system provides the current status of any book in the collection or student enrolled in the school. A librarian's notes can be sorted in the micro through a notepad feature. A complete and automatic backup system is included with ALS.

In developing ALS, Graham found that her team was ahead of its time. The biggest problem in implementing the system was waiting for the improvement of hard disk storage technology. When all the equipment had been acquired, Graham had a problem finding a location for it. She discovered that the intended location—next to a gas furnace—caused some distortions in the programs stored on the hard disk, because of the magentic field around the furnace's pilot light.

ALS was originally developed for use on a TRS-80 Model III featuring 48K memory and DOS operating system. The library has since made the software compatible with the IBM personal computer. Funding for the project came initially from ESEA IV-C, which provided $13,500. Additional monies were later provided by ECIA Chapter 2 and by the County Board of Education. Graham estimates Point Pleasant has spent about $33,500 on the project, which includes expenditures for the hardware and salaries for the consultant and student assistant.

To help offset costs, Point Pleasant has begun selling ALS to other interested schools. Through early spring 1984, the school had installed three systems for TRS-80s, had orders for eight more and had received six orders for programs to use with IBM machines. Cost of the system is $3000, which includes installation, training and consulting services.

To evaluate the effectiveness of ALS, Point Pleasant conducted a survey measuring the amount of time it took to do certain library functions with ALS and with manual methods. The results are given in Table 6 following.

Future roles for ALS include audiovisual control and, more immediately, an interlibrary loan system. Graham hopes to have an interlibrary loan system established with other Mason County schools by the winter of 1984–85. Student use of ALS is also expected to increase. At present they use the program only for reference searches. (The library also houses additional TRS-80s and Apples for use in computer-assisted instruction programs.)

Table 6: Point Pleasant Survey Results

Library Function	Manual Method (Mean Seconds)	Computer Method (Mean Seconds)
Check in books	62.4	35.5
Check out books	73.3	42.4
Assess daily fines	518.5	92.5
Locate borrower	100.6	6.8
Issue overdue notices	75.0	22.0
Payment of fines	98.0	37.0
Call number	82.8	14.3
Reference search	1084.0	308.0

Interest in ALS from other libraries has been tremendous, Graham says. In fact the inquiries regarding the system have been so great that Graham now uses a micro for another purpose—word processing—in an attempt to respond to all queries.

PORTSMOUTH PUBLIC LIBRARY
Portsmouth, NH

Type of library: Public
Size of population: 26,000
Type of population: General public
Micros owned: 4 Commodore VIC 20s, 2 Apple II+s, 1 Apple IIe
Software packages owned: VisiFile, VisiCalc, WordStar, PFS, PFS:
    Report, Mailmerge
Software developed in-house: None
Languages supported: BASIC
Operating systems: Apple DOS, CP/M

The Portsmouth Public Library has a total of seven micros: 4 "circulating" VIC 20s, a public access Apple II+, a second Apple II+ plus an Apple IIe for library administrative use.

In an attempt to allow patrons to familiarize themselves with micros, Portsmouth began a microcomputer loan program in February 1983. The library started the program with two VIC 20s, acquired through the library trust fund, and subsequently added two more VIC 20s through a donation from the local computer dealer who had sold the library its Apples. Under the program, a patron may borrow a VIC 20 for a two-week period. There is a $25 cash deposit at the time the computer is picked up, $10 of which is kept by the library as a usage fee. The balance of the deposit is refunded upon the return of the micro, on time, with all items in working order. To borrow the micro, a patron must be at least 21 years old, a borrower in good standing and have two forms of identification in addition to a library card. The borrower must also sign a contract in which he or she agrees to pay for any losses or damages. The late charge is $10 for the first day and $5 for each additional day. The loan package includes the computer, a cassette player, manuals, an instruction sheet on how to hook the micro to the TV and five programs, including games, business, home and word processing applications.

The loan program has been extremely well received by the public, and the library has had only minor problems. One early problem was solved after the library received the two donated micros. With only two micros, the library had been unable to fill requests quickly enough, and had considered ending its reserve policy in favor of a first-come, first-served policy. The two additional micros, however, alleviated the problem. Breakdown of the hardware has occurred infrequently, and the library has been able to have minor repairs made at a local vocational-technical college for free. Theft has been virtually non-existent; the library reports that no software, books or manuals have turned up "lost."

The Apple II+ available for public access is located next to Portsmouth's circulation desk. Initially located in the reference room, the Apple was moved because of the noise and crowds it generated. At its new location the Apple is "loosely overseen" by the circulation department. The staff gives only basic instruction on how to operate the micro (e.g., how to turn it on and insert the disk drive). It is then up to the operator to learn how to use the micro. Patrons using programs other than games may use the micro for one hour; game users are restricted to a half hour. There is no initial training prerequisite for using the micro, and all use it free.

Portsmouth has had only minor problems with the public access Apple. The library has lost only one program since the Apple was purchased in April 1982 and there have been no disk malfunctions. The keyboard has been replaced three times and the Silentype printer has been repaired once.

To further encourage public use of the micros, the library hired an outside computer consultant to conduct two computer courses during winter 1983. One course was an eight-week introduction to BASIC programming, the other was a hands-on computer workshop. Both courses were popular with the public; 188 people attended the 17 hands-on workshops. Fees were $3 for the workshop and $20 for the BASIC course.

For administrative functions, Portsmouth has found the Apple IIe most beneficial for word processing tasks. The library uses WordStar and Mailmerge software for general word processing tasks as well as to generate mailing lists, labels and periodicals listings.

VisiFile is used by the technical service department for acquisitions. The acquisitions program has proved a bit cumbersome in that it takes six disks to operate, requiring the disks to be popped in and out. The books are ordered on one disk and the printout is sent to the book jobber. The orders are then transferred to the main file, which is divided up alphabetically by author. The main file is purged every four to six months, and a list of unreceived books is routed to the appropriate librarian for a decision on reordering.

PFS and PFS: Report software are used for monitoring certain aspects of the library's inventory. The software monitors the inventory of books ordered to fill multiple reserves on bestsellers, as well as the inventory of the Seacoast Fiction Depository, a last-copy fiction depositor for New Hampshire Seacoast area libraries. The file is on eight disks and can print out an alphabetical listing by author of the entire collection of each library, as well as a list of the books each library has contributed to the depository. Computer software and hardware inventory is also on PFS.

Although the Portsmouth Library is becoming increasingly involved with micros, computer training continues to be conducted haphazardly. The bulk of the library staff members' computer education has been on the job. Formal training classes have been limited to a two-hour session at the computer store where the Apples were bought. The library did hire a local computer consultant to train seven staff members to use the word processing software. Some other staff members attended the library-sponsored computer workshops on their own initiative. Sue McCann, who oversees the library's micro activities as part of her job as assistant library director, reports that one of her major frustrations is not having enough time to properly educate herself, as well as the rest of the library staff, about the micros and their various capabilities. "It is very time consuming to learn the programs and to create files," she says. As an example of the time pressures, McCann explains that Portsmouth would "very much like to put its budget on VisiCalc," but has been unable to find the time to do so.

Through early 1984, Portsmouth had spent a total of just under $21,000 on hardware and software. Almost all of the money came from the library's trust fund with the exception of some of the software funds, which were donated by the Friends of the Portsmouth Library Association.

PROVIDENCE PUBLIC LIBRARY
Providence, RI

Type of library: Public
Size of population: 947,000
Type of population: General public
Micros owned: 1 Apple II+, 1 Apple IIe, 1 North Star Horizon, 4 Commodore 64s, 1 Eagle PC, 3 IBM Displaywriters
Software packages owned: LOGO, Inform, Search-Helper
Software developed in-house: Word processing and use-statistics management
Languages supported: BASIC, LOGO
Operating systems: MS DOS 1.0, Apple DOS 3.3, CP/M

"Haphazard" and "ad hoc" are two terms that could best describe the early microcomputer experience at the Providence Public Library. As the above list suggests, the library has acquired different micros for specific purposes in a process that Dick Desroches, assistant librarian for data processing, admits was very unorganized. To provide a more uniform micro program, Providence hired Desroches in early 1983, and Desroches has set the standardization of the micro operation as a top priority for Providence. However, implementation of a more standardized program has been slow, since the library has a limited budget for the acquisition of new software. Nonetheless, the library says it is committed to improving its micro program.

Despite the wide mixture of machines, micros have proved useful in several different applications at Providence. One of the more creative applications has been the use of the library's Eagle. Situated in the periodical room, the Eagle uses a CP/M operating system and a software package called Search-Helper for searching Dialog databases. The program quizzes a patron about the upcoming search before going on-line with Dialog. The Eagle then formulates the search strategy, connects with Dialog and retrieves the information. Using the Eagle saves time and money, with Providence estimating an average search cost of $2.50. Several members of the library's reference department staff are able to use the Eagle program, and it has also proved to be very popular with patrons. However, the program has not been trouble free. The most frequently voiced complaint is that the subhead titles presented at the start of the search do not accurately reflect what is actually called up.

Despite the popularity of search program, there is enough free time for the library to consider using the Eagle for other purposes. The most likely application will be to use the Eagle as a dumb terminal in an in-house circulation system.

Another application involves the library's North Star Horizon micro. Providence has placed two touch-screen display terminals in the building, one near the card catalog on the main floor, and one on the second floor. Using Inform software, the screens display general information about the library such as library hours, where the different departments are located, where the rest rooms are and how to use the card catalog. The screens can also display information on special library events and children's activities. In fact, the library has found that it has programmed more news for children than it had planned because the terminals are used more by kids than adults. Overall reaction to the terminals has been mixed, with some patrons believing there are cheaper ways to get this type of information across. The reluctance of adults to use the terminals has resulted in less use of these micros than Providence had anticipated.

Providence's Apple II+ is used to run the library's Micro 600 Port Selector in conjunction with Providence's CLSI circulation system. The Apple is used as a controlling terminal for the Port Selector and is kept as a separate unit, providing backup in the event that Providence's minicomputer fails.

The Apple IIe was originally acquired for remote database searching. However, the library has not used the micro for that purpose, and instead has used the IIe for general management functions including word processing and statistical management, with programs developed by Desroches.

The four Commodore 64 micros, which were acquired through a federal grant, are public access micros located in children's rooms in some of Providence's branch libraries. Use of Commodores is limited to children, who are encouraged to experiment on the machines and to familiarize themselves with the computers. The library provides a limited amount of software, including some game packages. Computer time is free, but time is generally limited to 30 minutes.

The three IBM Displaywriters were the first machines acquired by the library and are used solely for word processing. Located in the library director's office, the IBMs are valuable for fundraising campaigns—creating mailing lists and generating letters.

One problem with the Providence program has been inadequate funding. Desroches says he is "trying desperately" to get software added to the library's budget. An allocation of $1000 could provide Providence with some more basic software packages such as word processing and spreadsheet packages necessary for an efficient program. To save money, Providence has been using programs developed in-house by Desroches. However, Desroches hopes this attitude will change. It is often difficult to get library contributors to donate money for software, a product which is much less visible than hardware. Through the early part of 1984 Providence spent more than $10,000 on hardware but only a few hundred dollars on software.

Monetary restrictions have also limited Providence's in-house training efforts. Training has largely been limited to instruction by Desroches, who reports that staff reception to micros has been divided "pretty much along age lines," with staff members over 35 more reluctant to use the machines than their younger counterparts.

Providence has allocated funds for maintenance, although policy varies from micro to micro. In cases where the library feels it cannot be without the micro for a long period of time, it has signed maintenance contracts. One such contract, costing about $250 per year, is on the Eagle. Repairs on the Eagle generally take no longer than 24 hours, an important consideration for what has become an indispensable library tool.

SALT LAKE COUNTY LIBRARY SYSTEM
Salt Lake City, UT

Type of library: Public
Size of population: 480,000
Type of population: General public
Micros owned: 10 Apple IIes, 10 Franklins, 1 IBM PC
Software packages owned: Numerous educational games and application software packages
Software developed in-house: None

Languages supported: BASIC
Operating systems: DOS

By summer 1984 an **IBM PC** was the only microcomputer the Salt Lake County Library System was still using for staff functions. However, the lack of in-house applications does not mean that micros do not play an important role in the overall operating structure of the library system. The county system conducts an extensive public access micro program, a program that was begun when the library upgraded its automation system.

Micros were first introduced in Salt Lake when the library installed a CLSI system. Apples served as backup to that system and were also adapted for other uses such as word processing and database management. However, in early 1984 the library replaced the micros with an integrated Wang system. Using the Wang will allow the library to tie into other Utah government agency and university databases while still giving the library word processing and database management functions that had been provided by the Apples. The **IBM PC** is used for applications such as scheduling and statistics development.

With the Apples no longer needed for in-house applications, Salt Lake decided to use the micros in a public access program. The library has 10 Apples and 10 Franklin micros (which are compatible with the Apples) located in branches throughout the system, and expects to add 10 more Apple-compatible machines. The micros are available for use by patrons of all ages during regular library hours.

The operation of the Salt Lake public access program is more informal than many similar projects at other libraries. The library keeps no record of who has taken orientation classes, issues no cards identifying patrons who are permitted to use the machines and does not keep formal statistics of computer use. On the other hand Salt Lake has a degree of sophistication most other libraries do not enjoy in that the Apples are connected to several commercial databases, such as Dialog and Information Access, which patrons are encouraged to use.

It is the hope of Salt Lake officials that the micros can be used as information tools and not just playthings, according to Dale Jensen, coordinator of hardware acquisitions for the library system. In the first 18 months of the program, Jensen estimates that 80%–90% of micro use was for personal computing such as game playing, educational game playing and statistical management. The library encourages patrons who are considering buying software to use its facilities to evaluate different programs and to see which packages best fit their needs. Some area businesspeople use the micros for their own recordkeeping purposes, bringing in their own disks to run on the library's machines.

The library owns upward of 60 software titles ranging from educational games to spreadsheet packages. The library does not stock video games, but will allow patrons to bring in their own games during specified hours. Salt Lake charges $1 an hour for using the micro or $.25 for 15 minutes. No time limits are placed on patron use, and patrons may reserve time as often as they want during the week. The machines are in use an estimated 40%–50% of the time. Interested micro users are encouraged to attend computer workshops before using the micros, but attendance is not mandatory. The workshops are conducted on different levels, from teaching patrons how to boot the programs (inserting the disk to start the program) to demonstrating how to use spreadsheet functions. Jensen admits that teaching patrons how to use the micros is where the Salt Lake program "breaks down a bit." The library would like to have more regular workshop dates as well as more staff at branch libraries who are knowledgeable about micros.

The library has been frustrated in its efforts to offer software for circulation because of a lack of available funds. Although the library does own most major software packages, it does not want to start lending packages until it can acquire duplicate programs. The library does make available some public domain software for at-home use by patrons.

Otherwise Salt Lake has generally been able to get all the funding it needs to finance it micro program. Jensen estimates that Salt Lake has spent between $15,000 and $20,000 on software for its public access program and expects to spend another $10,000 in 1985. Hardware costs have run between $20,000 and $30,000. Financing for the micros was part of the regular library budget, although the 10 Franklins, received in early 1984, were acquired through a corporate donation. Salt Lake has actively sought corporate help in funding the micro program, with the Franklin micro donation the first tangible result of its efforts.

Salt Lake's micros are maintained by the system's audiovisual technician. Although the library has not had a service contract, it may get one if it significantly expands the program by acquiring new micros or increasing patron use. Repair problems have been held to a minimum in 1984, largely because the library stopped using its Atari machines. "The Ataris just didn't hold up as well as the Apples," Jensen says, noting that when the machines did need repair it was necessary to bring the micros to an Atari dealer, whereas in many cases an Apple could be fixed by the library's technician. In addition to breaking down more often than the Apples, the Ataris presented Salt Lake with a much tougher security problem in that the machines' peripherals were much easier to steal than the Apples' peripherals.

The public access program has been well supported by Salt Lake patrons, and the library believes that the $1 charge has not been a major obstacle in drawing people to the program. Jensen acknowledged that the library had not intended to charge for using the micro, but was driven to by political pressures. The charge was instituted to deflect criticism that micros were an unneccesary frill that the library cannot afford. The dollar fee allows the library to argue that the patrons who are interested in using the micros are helping to finance the program.

STANDARD & POOR'S CORP.
New York, NY

Type of library: Corporate
Size of population: 700
Type of population: Stock market analysts
Micros owned: 4 TRS-80 Model 12s
Software packages owned: Scripsit, VisiCalc, Multiplan, Profile
Software developed in-house: None
Languages supported: BASIC
Operating systems: DOS 2.0

A relative newcomer to microcomputers, Standard & Poor's has steadily added applications since it acquired its first TRS-80s in late 1983. The company adopted an approach of immediately using the machines for small applications while developing longer range major applications.

The small applications include word processing, budget planning and database management. Scripsit is used for word processing functions including letter writing, report generation and memos. A large portion of Standard & Poor's 20-person library staff is familiar with word processing. VisiCalc and Multiplan are used primarily by Dennis Jensen, corporate librarian, for budget planning. Jensen feels the microcomputer allows him to prepare the department's budget quicker, gives him a better understanding of the whole budget picture and permits him to make changes at the last minute. Profile software is used by several different people on the library staff to create small databases. One database was a file of the 400 Standard & Poor's subscribers to *The Wall Street Journal*.

A larger, more important database has been created in the library's central inquiry unit. The unit answers questions from customers for a fee. In the past, the unit recorded and billed all customers by hand, a somewhat lengthy process. With the TRS-80, the company now has a computerized list of its customers, records the number of inquiries made by each customer per month and prints out a bill for services on a monthly basis.

All of the smaller applications of the micro have permitted the library staff to do more work with no additional staff. "We can work smarter and more efficiently with the addition of the micros," says Jensen.

Standard & Poor's first major application is the development of the corporate file information system. The information center is being designed to automate a complicated system of acquiring checking-in and routing disclosure documents filed with the Securities and Exchange Commission by some 10,000 to 11,000 companies. Documents include annual and quarterly reports as well as 10-K filings. To date, the routing of documents has been done strictly by hand, occupying 12 people full time with documents stored in 100 five-drawer cabinets and on 1 million pieces of microfiche. When a document arrives at Standard & Poor's it is checked in and a 5 x 8 index card is attached to it. Then it is sent to another department where it is assigned to the proper analyst. Using the micro, Standard & Poor's hopes to be able to check in the documents more quickly and accurately as well as to speed up the routing process. With the micro, the analyst in charge of a particular company will be recorded at the information center, making the step of sending the indexed document out of the department for assignment to the proper analyst unnecessary.

The major barrier to completing the project has been loading the information. Standard & Poor's "didn't want a small army in the office keying in entries," Jensen reports, so the library cast about for an in-house database that had most of the names the library needed. After some weeks of searching, a database was found that was thought to contain about 90% of the necessary names. It then took a few months for the library to read the tape, using a DEC minicomputer, to make sure it was the right one. The library discovered, however, that the tape was indeed the wrong one, adding to the delay. After finally acquiring the correct database, the next time-consuming process was the transfer of the information on to eight-inch floppy disks, and then the transfer of the material into a Profile system. The transfer problem was compounded by the fact that the library's programmer was unfamiliar with Radio Shack language and had to learn on the job.

Despite the problems, by summer 1984 the project was well under way. As originally planned three TRS-80s will be used as workstations and a fourth will serve as a storage computer. The system will be networked through Arcnet.

The ability of the Radio Shack machines to be used in a local area network was the deciding factor in Standard & Poor's choice of the TRS-80s. At the time it was investigating micros, Radio Shack provided the best networking capabilities at the best price. Reliability of performance was another factor in choosing the TRS-80s, and the company has not had any problems in the short amount of time it has been using the machines. The company has, nonetheless, taken a service contract on the micros. "It's difficult to take a risk with that much equipment," Jensen notes, adding that the technical staff recommended the contract. Standard & Poor's has invested some $27,000 in the micro program.

The use of the micros has also helped the Standard & Poor's library staff keep abreast of state-of-the-art developments in library science. Because corporate policy calls for only one librarian to conduct online searches, other staff members had started to feel a little behind in the latest developments. This situation has been resolved with the introduction of the micros, Jensen says, since those librarians who are not conducting online searches can still use the micros for such tasks as word processing and acquisitions.

TOWER HILL SCHOOL LIBRARY
Wilmington, DE

Type of library: School
Size of population: 680
Type of population: Faculty and students
Micros owned: 1 Apple IIe
Software packages owned: VisiCalc, Bank Street Writer, Data Capture,
    Overdue Writer, PFS: File, PFS: Report, PFS: Graph
Software developed in-house: None
Languages supported: BASIC, LOGO
Operating systems: DOS

Microcomputers are part of the entire learning process at Tower Hill School. The school owns a total of 12 micros with one Apple IIe, acquired in 1983, dedicated specifically to library use. Of the remaining machines, 10 are for student use and one is for teacher use. The student micros are located in a special room within the library. Some of the money for the micros came from the annual Tower Hill School mothers' clothing drive, with matching funds donated by a school trustee. A portion of the audiovisual budget has also been used to acquire software.

Although Nancy Minnich, head librarian at Tower Hill, is now satisfied with her Apple IIe, she was not always a fan of the Apple family. Minnich felt the original Apple had too many restrictions, with the inability to go to 80 columns a particular annoyance. The IIe, however, meets the needs of the library and also provides a useful teaching tool for students. According to Minnich, Bank Street Writer can be taught quickly and easily, thus encouraging students to use the micro, whereas Scripsit, for use on the school's TRS-80, proved too difficult for the children to handle.

In general, Minnich finds Apple-compatible software more helpful for educating students. This is an important consideration for Minnich who, in conjunction with teachers, has taught word processing to eighth graders and has also taught students how to search Dialog databases. Despite Minnich's involvement in teaching students, she does not believe the school library should be the place where micros are used for remedial work. Rather, she has become involved with the computer education of students in an attempt to give them the widest possible access to information.

For administrative purposes, Minnich uses her Apple IIe for "every bit of communication" that is generated by her office. Letters and articles are written using Bank Street Writer software, while mailing lists are created using Profile programs. Profile has also been used to create small bibliographies. The library has been using VisiCalc to monitor its budget, but Minnich decided that program was "too powerful" for the library's needs. Instead, VisiCalc is being used by several teachers to monitor data in a study of gifted and talented students. For budgetary matters the school library is planning to use Dollars and Sense software. Data Capture software has been used in some early interlibrary loan and database searching efforts, and Minnich hopes to expand these areas in the future. Book orders are placed with Bro-Dart using the micro and Bookrack software.

The library's micro was also used to "open the door" for Tower Hill's involvement in networking. Tower Hill has been a member of Palinet/OCLC since 1982. The first year in which Tower Hill had a full membership in Palinet it used its micro to access the OCLC database. In its second year of membership, Minnich wrote a LSCA grant for Title III money to establish a consortium with an OCLC dumb terminal. Although Minnich concedes this approach is more cost-effective than accessing OCLC through a micro, she explains that it was the micro that enabled Tower Hill to become involved with networking in the first place. The further use of micros as a telecommunications tool is something that Minnich wants very much to explore.

Minnich is convinced that micros have been, and can continue to be, important tools for school librarians for a relatively low cost. Tower Hill's Apple IIe, complete with 80-column card, Epson printer and green monitor, cost $2200. The school has spent approximately $1000 on software materials that are used by the library, students and teachers.

Minnich has found that in addition to providing greater efficiency in library tasks and encouraging increased student use of the library, the micro has also helped to "change the tenor of the use of the library" by teachers as well. The micro helped the library get the attention of teachers and made them conscious of the fact that the library is more than just a place where books are stored, Minnich explains. "The micro has given the library a better image and made it easier to sell our services."

UNIVERSITY OF PENNSYLVANIA LIBRARIES
Philadelphia, PA

Type of library: University
Size of population: 20,000
Type of population: Faculty, students, researchers
Micros owned: 8 IBM PCs, 1 IBM PC/XT, 1 Apple II+, 5 DEC
    Rainbows
Software packages owned: FinalWord, Multimate, Volkswriter, Lotus
    1-2-3, PFS: File, PFS: Report, PFS: Graph, PFS: Write, Knowl-
    edge Manager, packages for asynchronous communications
Software developed: Some BASIC programs for Management informa-
    tion systems (MIS)
Languages supported: BASIC
Operating systems: Apple DOS 3.3, PC DOS

Microcomputers play an important part in expanding the services
offered by the University of Pennsylvania libraries and are expected
to play an even larger role in the future. The overall direction of the
micro program is being forged by the library director, Richard De Gen-
naro, while the day to day operation is overseen by Roy Heinz, who
also supervises the library's minicomputer operations. An important
step in formatting a micro plan for the future was the decision by the
director to make IBM the standard micro for Penn's main library. The
knowledge that IBM "will be around" to support the machines was
the most important consideration in selecting the PCs, according to
Heinz.

Penn uses the micros for three main applications: database management, word processing and spreadsheet analysis. Database management has been the application most widely used in the library. Different departments have used PFS software to create a number of new,
small databases. Penn houses the papers of Theodore Dreiser, and has
used an IBM to catalog all of Dreiser's correspondence. The library
has classified all the letters written to Dreiser by name of author and
by the year in which they were written. Penn is also conducting an oral
history of chemistry, using the micros to transcribe recorded interviews
with famous chemists. Later, it will use micros to index the collection.

A Friends of the Library list has been entered onto the eight IBMs,
which allows Penn to produce lists according to different categories

(such as donors of more than $1000). The circulation department uses the micros to keep track of the names of delinquent patrons, record the different stages of the collection process, and track the amount of fines owed to the library. Cataloging and editing librarians use the micro to change main entries. Personnel files are also kept up-to-date with the IBM.

Despite the many different applications of PFS: File, in early summer 1984 Penn decided to standardize its database management using Knowledge Manager, a software program that Penn believes is more powerful than the PFS family. Penn plans to develop larger, more extensive databases with Knowledge Manager. PFS software will still be used for smaller applications.

The library has been using four different word processing packages: Multimate, PFS: Write, Volkswriter and FinalWord. Multimate is being used by staff members who were familiar with Wang word processing, since the Multimate commands are similar to those of Wang. People using word processing for the first time are usually taught on Volkswriter and PFS: Write, since these programs are easier to use than FinalWord. Although Penn would like to standardize the word processing system, it does not want to push people into using a program they may not be comfortable with.

Lotus 1-2-3 is used by the business office for budget analysis, while the circulation department uses Lotus for statistics gathering. The library's work-study program is also monitored by Lotus.

The IBM asynchronous communications package is used by Penn to link its micros to its mainframe and minicomputers. Because Penn's minicomputer has no utilities that permit sorting, Penn has found it very beneficial to download materials to its micros; the materials can then be sorted out in any order the library wishes. A planned Penn Information Network will also invoice micros linked to the campus mainframe. Scheduled to be developed over the next five years, the campus-wide information network, of which the library will be just one part, will be mainframe-based with micros serving a supporting role.

The library's Apple II+ was acquired to serve as a backup for Penn's CLSI turnkey circulation system. The Apple was the first micro bought by the library, but Penn has no plans to add any additional functions to the machine. An IBM PC/XT is used by the reference department to store long documents.

Penn's business school library, which is housed in the same building as the main university library, recently acquired five DEC Rainbow micros. The Rainbows, which were donated to the library, will be used in conjunction with the business school library's DEC minicomputer.

Penn's hardware was acquired through donations and from general library funds and software monies were provided by the library's general budget for automation. In the future Penn hopes to establish a formal micro budget, and hopes to add a number of new micros to its current roster. At present only a small number of the library staff has access to micros and Penn would like to encourage broader use. A series of workshops and training sessions are being planned for library staff members, and the library is also getting involved with on-campus computer users organizations.

WAYNE STATE UNIVERSITY LIBRARIES
Detroit, MI

Type of library: University
Size of population: 30,000
Type of population served: Students and faculty
Micros owned: 5 Apple II+s, 8 Osbornes
Software packages owned: WordStar, SuperCalc, dBase II, Screen Pac
Software developed in-house: Library location guide
Languages supported: BASIC
Operating systems: CP/M

Wayne State has a long history of using computers in its university libraries, dating back to 1963. Its experience with microcomputers is much more recent, beginning in June 1982 when the director of libraries approved the purchase of an Apple II+. The first Apple was used in a program designed by Wayne State to provide an opportunity for its library staff to learn how to use micros, and to examine the machines for possible applications in the library system. As outlined by library officials, the testing program would last from June 1982 to September 1983.

To ensure that the library would gain the most accurate results from the test, the library established several procedural steps it planned to follow. The first of these steps was the attendance of the library director and assistant director at some BASIC programming classes, with the assistant director continuing with programming classes in VisiCalc, WordStar and DB Master. Then a four-hour introductory class on micro use was developed for the entire library staff. The class suggested 13 follow-up activities staff members could engage in to develop their understanding of how to use micros. About 60% of the library staff signed up for the classes.

Soon after the acquisition of the Apple, library officials determined that to facilitate the micro education of the staff, a micro would be bought for each of the six library units on campus. After a study of different proposals, the decision was made to acquire Osborne micros. The selection of the Osborne was based on the fact that it was equipped with three major software programs: WordStar, SuperCalc and dBase II. Library officials believed these software programs would provide the staff with an opportunity to quickly learn to use micros and apply them to library needs. At this point, the Osbornes were seen primarily as a learning and development tool. As applications were developed, proposals were to be written and submitted for a micro that could meet the needs of a particular application.

Wayne State library officials believed a number of benefits would evolve from the test period. Officials hoped that by using the micros, the staff would become computer literate and would increase their understanding of the capabilities, potentials and shortcomings of computing. By using various software packages, the library staff was expected to begin the development of different library applications. By analyzing the normal work routines to see if they could be computerized, the staff was expected to develop analytical skills to assist them in improving operations. Officials believed this was important to learn, ''since 80% of the work of designing an application for a micro involves analysis of the work to be done.''

To conduct the test program Wayne State bought a total of eight Osbornes, with related materials. Despite some problems, the most serious of which was the collapse of the Osborne Computer Co., Wayne State managed to follow the guidelines it had established for setting up a micro program. (The guidelines are reproduced in Figure 1.) The library identified three main applications of use for the micros—word process-

Figure 1: Wayne State Guidelines for a Micro Program

STEPS IN IMPLEMENTING A MICROCOMPUTER PROGRAM
1. Become personally committed
2. Become personally knowledgeable
3. Identify the key people
4. Identify tools and techniques to use
5. Develop an action plan with dates
6. Communicate with everyone throughout the whole program
7. Publicize the program
8. Monitor the progress of the program—refining
9. Think of what lies ahead—renewing
10. Evaluate the program

KEY DECISION MAKERS
1. President, Provost of the University
2. Director/Dean of Libraries
3. Middle management library staff
4. Librarians
5. Library para-professionals/technicians
6. Library clerks
7. Purchasing department
8. Computing Center
9. You, yourself

TOOLS AND TECHNIQUES
1. Cost comparisons of microcomputers
2. Analysis of advantages and disadvantages of various microcomputers
3. Criteria for selecting a microcomputer
4. Benefits of buying a microcomputer
5. A program
6. Find allies
7. Point to other examples of libraries using microcomputers
8. Attitude survey
9. Training program
10. Rewards

ing, spreadsheet analysis and database management. In addition, the library has decided that in the future it will use IBM PCs in its programs.

While the IBMs are on order, Wayne State continues to use the Osbornes it acquired in November 1982. WordStar software is used by members of the staff for standard word processing functions. Any staff member who wishes to use the micro for word processing may do so, provided they sign up in advance. The library also permits staffers to take the Osbornes home at night.

The library's business officer has been the primary person using the micro for spreadsheet purposes. Using SuperCalc, the business officer does budget analysis on the micro. An early application was using the micro to keep track of vacant library positions and then to measure the savings in salaries. Another use has been to monitor new orders of serials as well as canceled subscriptions. The Osbornes are also used to control the budget of the library's serials union list. Database management functions have been minimally explored, with the only program of any significance a listing of supplies by the audiovisual department.

The library has also acquired four more Apple II + s since its initial acquisition in 1982. Three of the machines are used as part of a library micro lab for student use, while two Apples are used in conjunction with the library's library location guide, developed by a Wayne State reference librarian. Using the library location guide, patrons can key in the call number of a book, and the micro will tell them where in the building the book is located. The program is in use in two campus library units, and has worked well. The major problem in developing the program was determining what wrong entries the patrons would make and what response would be necessary to get them back on track.

WESTERN ILLINOIS UNIVERSITY LIBRARY
Macomb, IL

Type of library: University
Size of population: 18,000
Type of population: Students, faculty
Micros owned: 5 Apple II + s, 3 Apple IIes, 1 Lisa, 1 IBM PC/XT
Software packages owned: WordStar, dBase II, Screen Writer
Software developed in-house: None
Languages supported: BASIC
Operating systems: CP/M, DOS

The nature of microcomputer use at the Western Illinois University Library has changed significantly since the first micros were acquired in 1981. The first Apple II+ was bought in conjunction with a Nestar hard disk for the generation and operation of an electronic billboard system throughout the library's new building. The library was looking for a way to "catch people's eyes about news of the library," according to assistant director Del Williams, and decided that a series of small display screens placed throughout the building would be the most effective method. Use of the billboard system allows the library to use graphics in its presentations and to change messages quickly if the need arises. Messages are usually changed once a week. The billboard displays news of upcoming library events as well as general information items. The operation of the program is overseen by the library's audiovisual staff.

Reaction to the billboard system has been positive among the library's patrons, and the library continues to employ it, although it is now considered the least important aspect of the library's use of micros. As the billboard system was being established, Western Illinois quickly realized that micros could be used for more ambitious projects. The library bought six additional Apples and created a local area network using a bus with the Nestar.

The development of the LAN "easily fell into place," Williams said. The LAN uses one Apple to control the Nestar hard disks with six other Apples directly wired to the Nestar. Each Apple features different types of equipment, with one station, for instance, having a daisy wheel printer and another a disk drive. Virtual diskettes (an operating system that expands the memory capacity of a micro) are another featured part of the system since they allow for the creation of longer files and a minimum amount of "jockeying" for disks, Williams explains. The primary benefit of the LAN is that it permits the transfer of data from one terminal to another, allowing the library to maximize use of its existing equipment at a relatively low cost. To date, Western Illinois has limited the LAN to the library building only, but has discussed the possibility of distributing CP/M software by a telecom link throughout the campus, thus linking the library to other micros on campus.

Primarily using WordStar software, the LAN is used for standard word processing tasks such as the generation of letters, reports and articles. It is the creation of new databases, and the extension of existing databases, however, that has proved the greatest benefit to Western Illinois. dBase II is the software most often used by the library to create and manage its databases. In the database field, micros have been particularly helpful in the special collections area creating "files that we should have had before, but didn't have the ability to develop," says Williams. The library has created a small collection catalog of its holdings of plays and photographs, as well as an index for its collection of the papers of former Congressman Thomas Railsback (Rep.-IL). dBase II is also used by the library in the creation of a campus-wide directory of software. The first software directory was developed by the library in 1983, and a second edition was being readied in 1984. In addition, dBase II is used in the creation of bibliographies.

The micro program is run by three people—a hardware expert, a programmer and a computer layman (Williams) who acts as unofficial coordinator of the micro program. Each of the three takes an active part in training other members of the library staff. According to Williams, Western Illinois had initially hired an outside consultant to conduct formal training sessions, but these sessions were abandoned in favor of informal, in-house training periods. "The formal sessions really didn't work very well," Williams notes. Rather, the library found that one-on-one training on a specific application was a far more effective tool for educating the staff. "Individual staff members would identify a need that they thought the use of a micro could fill, and we would then show them the correct application," Williams says. "You have to understand what people's opposition to micros is, and then show them why the opposition isn't warranted."

Western Illinois's commitment to using micros in the library is firm. The library has spent approximately $75,000 on hardware and software and plans to buy two to five more micros. The additional micros will most likely be Apples. The library feels the Apples provide a lot of operational flexibility at an affordable price. The Apples have had few operating problems, and the software has also met the library's expectations.

To date, the library has not used the micros for many spreadsheet functions, but anticipates adding these applications in the next school year. Patron usage of the machines has also been very limited, and Western Illinois has no definite plans for upgrading this part of its program. "We have more than 1000 computer science majors here, and if we can only make one micro available, I'm afraid it would be overrun and of questionable effectiveness," Williams says.

WIDENER UNIVERSITY LIBRARY
Wilmington, DE

Type of library: University
Size of population: 2000
Type of population: Students and faculty
Micros owned: 1 IBM PC
Software packages owned: PC File III, VisiCalc, VisiFile
Software developed in-house: None
Languages supported: BASIC
Operating systems: DOS

The library staff at the Delaware Campus of Widener University has engaged in a frenzy of activity since the library acquired its own IBM PC in spring 1984. "We've become PC junkies," librarian Jane Hukill says. The enthusiasm is understandable: During the 1983–84 academic year, the library housed a microcomputer lab, with 11 IBM PCs. For the most part, however, the library staff could only observe students using the micros and were unable to implement any of their own programs. That all changed in May 1984 when the university purchased an IBM for the library.

The micro was acquired by the college computer center, which acts as the purchasing agent for all computer acquisitions. The choice of the IBM had previously been made by university administrators, who decided that the IBM would be the school's micro. They believe the IBM is the micro students are most likely to encounter in the workplace.

The micro lab was created when the university declared that all incoming freshman must take an introduction to data processing course, and more computers for student use were needed. The library was chosen to house the lab because it offered tight security and long hours. Library staff did reap some benefits from the student lab. A few used the lab to learn some computer basics, and the library borrowed some software when it first acquired its own machine.

Among the first micro applications developed by the library for its own use were a catalog of audiovisual materials and a list of the faculty library collection. The library also created a new database of the menu collection of the university's restaurant school. Menus are listed by ethnic dish, city where the restaurant is located and restaurant name. Hukill reports that the use of the micro has aided the school's attempts to add more restaurants to its collection. Another early application was the creation of a master calendar of the library's activities. The software involved in all cases was PC File III, a "very simple to use, user-friendly software program," says Hukill.

PC File III was also used for the creation of a student hold list, developed at the end of the 1984 spring semester. It is used to delay grades or diplomas pending payment of any outstanding library fines. The use of the micro has permitted the library to be more efficient, and more accurate, in its holding program. It is also allowing the library to phase out paper records for student fines. In addition, the micro has improved the library's billing procedures for fines collection since the micro is tied into the college mainframe computer, which generates the actual billing notices.

During summer 1984 the library staff concentrated on putting all the repetitious work and all forms on disks, as well as exploring in more detail the word processing capabilities of the micro, using WordStar software. The staff also transferred its database and searching capabilities from its Commodore VIC to the IBM, since the IBM can provide for more sophisticated searches than the Commodore. The IBM will be used to access Information Access' Newsearch program.

WORCESTER PUBLIC LIBRARY
Worcester, MA

Type of library: Public
Size of population: 140,000
Type of population: General public
Micros owned: 2 Apple II + s, 1 Apple IIe
Software packages owned: VisiCalc, games
Software developed in-house: Page listing
Languages supported: BASIC, PASCAL
Operating systems: DOS

A true dichotomy exists in the microcomputer operations of the Worcester Public Library. The micro program for in-house administrative purposes operates on a highly decentralized, almost haphazard, basis, while the micros program in the children's room is run in a highly organized manner.

1984 was the third summer of Worcester's public access micro program for children, a program that features an Apple II + and is overseen by children's head librarian Carolyn Noah. Although Worcester considers the program a success, Noah admits that it is different from what the library had envisioned. Originally, the library wanted to provide a comprehensive computer literacy program for children. However, the program was a victim of its own success. Demand for the program became "too great" Noah says, necessitating a cutback in the program's goals. Worcester is now attempting to provide computer awareness to students. The program seeks to explain what a computer can do and how it operates, and to introduce some software programs, but nothing further. The library has the resources available if students wish to explore programming on their own, but the library has nothing official planned on a regular basis.

Another change in the program since its inception has been the demographics of the children using the micro. When the program began, the majority of the participants were affluent children who were serious computer users. Noah said that as these students acquired micros for use at home they were gradually replaced at the library by less affluent "street smart kids."

An estimated 1400 children have taken part in the program, and the demand has not slackened since its inception. Orientation classes of one hour are conducted by staff members on a rotating basis. All classes are free, as is participation in the program itself. Noah conducts some special classes in which she teaches LOGO.

Noah makes the purchasing decisions concerning software programs. The library has approximately 30 different packages, ranging from pure game materials to strictly educational programs. Funds for the software come from the children's department book budget.

Initially, Noah says, the implementation of the micro program was very demanding on the library staff. The burden was eased considerably as the library established set procedures for the children to follow. As the program operates now, the children are left alone with the micro after they complete the orientation program, although a librarian is always available to troubleshoot any problems. Although the program has operated without any major problems, Worcester is finding that as the children become more computer sophisticated, problems are more likely to occur. During summer 1984 Worcester experienced an increase in the copying and altering of disks.

The success of the public access program notwithstanding, there are no immediate plans for the library to increase its use of micros for administrative use, although Noah said she may attempt to create a bibliography on the machine.

The establishment of procedures helped ease the demands of the public access program, but the rest of the Worcester library has not yet standardized its procedures. The library started using micros in 1982, with staff members free to do as much or as little with the micros as they wished. As the program developed, no one person assumed overall responsibility for it. The library is now trying to correct this problem as it increases its commitment to micros in terms of both time and money. The lack of one computer leader, and shortages of overall staff time have been the major stumbling blocks in Worcester's attempts to increase its applications of micros quickly.

The immediate goal of the library is to cut down on the amount of redundant paper work. To this end, staff members have put different forms on disks and are using the Apples for statistical preparation. Worcester has also improved its label generation capability by using the micro. Use of the Apple allows the library to print only the labels it needs for a particular mailing, making the library's old address machine obsolete. The audiovisual department has used the Apple to inventory its supplies and has also written its own training program on how to operate different pieces of equipment. In another unrelated use of the micro, some library staff members have trained adults on the use of micros in free courses.

In the past, hardware and software acquisitions have been made by the head librarian, with recommendations by the automation committee. A more formal schedule of micro use will be established in the near future.

Part IV

Appendixes

Appendix A: Microcomputer Survey Questionnaire

Knowledge Industry Publications, Inc.   **White Plains, New York**

CASE STUDIES: MICROCOMPUTERS IN LIBRARIES
SURVEY OF USERS, FEBRUARY 1984

Dear Librarian:

Please fill out this questionnaire on your library's use of microcomputers. Information gathered from this survey will be used in a forthcoming book to be published by Knowledge Industry Publications, Inc. Please use additional sheets if necessary.

Name of library _____

Address _____

Telephone _____ Contact person_____

Population served (number & type, e.g., general public, professionals, students)_____

What kind(s) of micro does the library own?_____

How many?_____ Year(s) of purchase _____ Purchase price _____

What was included in the purchase price (e.g., peripherals, software)? _____
_____

Micro configuration:

Memory (K) _____   Operating system_____

External storage capacity (K) and type (tape, floppy disk, hard disk) _____
_____

Languages supported _____

Peripherals (e.g., printer) _____

Is the micro part of an integrated system? _____ If so, please describe. _____
_____

For what applications is the micro used?

_____Local data base searching   _____Remote data base searching

_____Circulation control/backup   _____Interlibrary loan

_____A/V control   _____Computer-assisted instruction

_____Serials control   _____Acquisitions

_____Online catalog   _____Local data base development

_____Reserve book room   _____Catalogs, lists, bibliographies

_____General management (e.g., word processing, fiscal control)

_____Other (please specify) _____

Is the micro available for patron use? _____ If so, for what purposes?_____
_____

What software packages do you own? _____
_____

Has the library developed its own software? _____ If so, please describe. _____
_____

Do you expect to purchase additional software? _____ If so, for what applications? _____
_____

Do you expect to develop your own software? _____ If so, for what applications? _____
_____

Please use the space below to describe your library's experiences with microcomputer use. Feel free to use additional sheets.

Appendix B: Directory of Libraries Profiled

Baptist Hospital Health Science Library
8900 N. Kendall Dr.
Miami, FL 33176
Contact: Diane Ream
Phone: 305-596-6506
Micro: Apple II+

Cordis Corp. Library
105555 W. Flagler St.
Miami, FL 33152
Contact: Sharyn Ladner
Phone: 305-551-2380
Micro: NCR Worksaver

Denver Public Library
1357 Broadway
Denver, CO 80202
Contact: William Campbell
Phone: 303-571-2000
Micros: Apple IIe, Apple II+, IBM PC/XT

Grace A. Dow Memorial Library
1710 W. St. Andrews Dr.
Midland, MI 48640
Contact: Randall Dykhuis
Phone: 517-835-7151
Micros: Apple II+, Franklin 1000

East Carolina University
Health Sciences Library
Brody Building
Greenville, NC 27834
Contact: Jo Ann Bell
Phone: 919-757-2214
Micros: Apple IIe, TRS-80 Model II, TRS-80 Model 12

Ekstrom Library
University of Louisville
Louisville, KY 40292
Contact: Sharon Edge
Phone: 502-588-6757
Micros: Apple II+, IBM PC/XT

Fairport Public Library
1 Village Landing
Fairport, NY 14450
Contact: Lisa Wemett
Phone: 716-223-9091
Micro: Apple II+

Clement C. Fry Collection
Yale Medical Library
333 Cedar St.
New Haven, CT 06510
Contact: Susan Wheeler
Phone: 203-785-4260
Micros: North Star Horizon, IBM PC/XT

Glendora Library and Cultural Center
140 S. Glendora Ave.
Glendora, CA 91740
Contact: John Jolly
Phone: 818-963-4160
Micros: IBM PC, IBM PC/XT, TRS-80
    Model III, Apple IIe, Eagle 1600

Monroe C. Gutman Library
Harvard University Graduate School of Education

6 Appian Way
Cambridge, MA 02138
Contact: Barbara Graham
Phone: 617-495-4228
Micros: Apple IIe, Apple II+, Digital Rainbow 100

Hershey Foods Corp. Communications Center
1025 Reese Ave.
PO Box 805
Hershey, PA 17033
Contact: Bill Woodruff
Phone: 717-534-5223
Micros: HP-125, IBM PC, OCLC 300

Kitsap Regional Library
1301 Sylvan Way
Bremerton, WA 98310
Contact: Michael Schuyler
Phone: 206-377-7601
Micros: Apple II, IBM PC

Lincoln Public Library
326 S. Seventh St.
Springfield, IL 62701
Contact: James LaRue
Phone: 217-753-4919
Micros: Apple II+, Apple IIe

Lorain Public Library
351 Sixth St.
Lorain, OH 44052
Contact: Valerie Smith
Phone: 216-244-1192
Micro: TRS-80 Model III

Maine State Library
Augusta, MA 04333
Contact: Donald Wismer
Phone: 207-289-3328
Micros: TRS-80 Model III, TRS-80 Model IV

Mansfield-Richland County Public Library
43 W. Third St.
Mansfield, OH 44902
Contact: Leslie Lee
Phone: 419-524-1041
Micro: TRS-80 Model III

Morris Library-Special Collections
Southern Illinois University
Carbondale, Il 62901
Contact: D.V. Koch
Phone: 618-453-2543
Micros: TRS-80 Model II, TRS-80 Model 100

Mudd Learning Center
Oberlin College
Oberlin, OH 44074
Contact: Katherine Frohmberg
Phone: 216-775-8285
Micros: Intel MDS, Osborne

National Agricultural Library
10301 Baltimore Blvd.
Beltsville, MD 20705
Contact: Philip Turner
Phone: 301-344-3813
Micros: Apple II, Compaq, IBM PC, Lanier, Alpha

National Bureau of Standards Library
E106 Administration Building
Washington, DC 20234
Contact: Marvin Brown
Phone: 301-921-3401
Micros: Apple II+, Seequa Chameleon, Kaypro II, Epson HX20

National Library of Canada
Public Services Branch
395 Weelington St.
Ottawa, Ont.

Canada K/A ON4
Contact: William Newman
Phone: 819-997-7000
Micros: IBM PC, Apple II+

North-Pulaski Branch Library
The Chicago Public Library
4041 W. North Ave.
Chicago, IL 60639
Contact: Marvin Garber
Phone: 312-235-2727
Micro: Apple II+

Novo Laboratories Library
59 Danbury Rd
Wilton, CT 06897
Contact: Jim Fleagle
Phone: 203-762-2401
Micro: Apple II

Plainfield Public Library
8th St. at Park Ave.
Plainfield, NJ 07060
Contact: Thomas Ballard
Phone: 201-757-1111
Micros: TRS-80 Model III, TRS-80
    Model II, TRS-80 Model 16B

Point Pleasant High School Library
2312 Jackson Ave.
Pt. Pleasant, WV 25550
Contact: Judy Graham
Phone: 304-675-4350
Micro: TRS-80 Model III

Portsmouth Public Library
8 Islington St.
Portsmouth, NH 03801
Contact: Sue McCann

Phone: 603-431-2000
Micros: Apple II+, Apple IIe, Commodore Vic 20

Providence Public Library
150 Empire St.
Providence, RI 02903
Contact: Doris Hornby
Phone: 401-521-8750
Micros: Apple II+, Apple IIe, North Star
    Horizon, Commodore 64, Eagle PC,
    IBM Displaywriter

Salt Lake County Library System
2197 E. 7000 St.
Salt Lake City, UT 84121
Contact: Dale Jensen
Phone: 801-943-4636
Micros: Apple IIe, Franklin, IBM PC

Standard & Poor's Corp.
25 Broadway
New York, NY 10004
Contact: Dennis Jensen
Phone: 212-208-8519
Micro: TRS-80 Model 12

Tower Hill School Library
2813 W. 17th St.
Wilmington, DE 19806
Contact: Nancy Minnich
Phone: 302-575-0550
Micro: Apple IIe

University of Pennsylvania Libraries
3420 Walnut St.
Philadelphia, PA 19104
Contact: Roy Heinz
Phone: 215-898-7094
Micros: Apple II+, IBM PC, IBM PC/XT, DEC Rainbow

Wayne State University Libraries
Detroit, MI 48202
Contact: Louise Bugg
Phone: 313-577-4058
Micros: Osborne, Apple II+

Western Illinois University Library
Macomb, IL 61455
Contact: Del Williams
Phone: 309-298-2411
Micros: Apple II+, Apple IIe, IBM PC/XT, Lisa

Widener University Library
Delaware Campus Library
Box 7139
Concord Pike
Wilmington, DE 19803
Contact: Jane Hukill
Phone: 302-478-3000
Micro: IBM/PC

Worcester Public Library
Salem Square
Worcester, MA 01608
Contact: Glenn Musser
Phone: 617-799-1672
Micros: Apple IIe, Apple II+

Appendix C: Selected Microcomputer Hardware and Software Vendors

HARDWARE

Alpha Micro
17332 Von Darman
PO Box 18347
Irvine, CA 92714

Apple Computer, Inc.
20525 Mariani Ave.
Cupertino, CA 95014

Atari, Inc.
1265 Borregas Ave.
Sunnyvale, CA 94086

Commodore Business Machines, Inc.
1200 Wilson Dr.
West Chester, PA 19380

Compaq Computer Corp.
20333 FM149
Houston, TX 77070

Digital Equipment Corp.
Continental Blvd.
Merrimack, NH 03054

Eagle Computer, Inc.
983 University Ave.
Los Gatos, CA 95030

Epson America, Inc.
23530 Hawthorne Blvd.
Torrance, CA 90505

Hewlett-Packard Co.
1010 NE Circle
Corvallis, OR 97330

IBM Corp.
Box 1325
Boca Raton, FL 33432

Intel Corp.
3065 Bowers Ave.
Santa Clara, CA 95051

Kaypro
533 Stevens Ave.
Solana Beach, CA 92075

Lanier Business Products
1700 Chantilly Drive NE
Atlanta, GA 30324

NCR Corp.
1700 S. Patterson Blvd.
Dayton, OH 45479

North Star Computers, Inc.
14440 Catalina St.
San Leandro, CA 94577

Radio Shack (division of
Tandy Corp.)
1800 One Tandy Dr.
Fort Worth, TX 76102

Seequa Computer Corp.
8305 Telegraph Rd.
Odenton, MD 21113

Vector Graphic, Inc.
500 N. Ventu Park Rd.
Thousand Oaks, CA 91320

SOFTWARE

Apple Computer
20525 Mariani Ave.
Cupertino, CA 95014
408-996-1010
Apple Writer

Ashton-Tate
10150 W. Jefferson Blvd.
Culver City, CA 90230
213-204-5570
dBase II

Broderbund Software
1938 4th St.
San Rafael, CA 94901
415-456-6424
Bank Street Writer

Computer Associates
125 Jericho Turnpike

Jericho, NY 11753
516-333-6700
Easywriter, SuperCalc

Control Data Corp.
PO Box O
8100 34th Ave. S.
Minneapolis, MN 55440
VisiCalc, VisiFile

Lifetree Software
411 Pacific St.
Suite 315
Monterey, CA 93940
408-373-4718
Volkswriter

Lotus Development Corp.
161 First St.
Cambridge, MA 02142

617-492-7171
Lotus 1-2-3

Micropro International Corp.
33 San Pablo Ave.
San Rafael, CA 94903
415-499-1200
WordStar, Mailmerge, Calcstar,
    Spellstar

Microsoft Corp.
10700 Northup Way
Bellevue, WA 98004
206-828-8080
Multiplan

MicroStuf, Inc.
1845 The Exchange
Suite 140
Atlanta, GA 30039
Crosstalk

Multimate International Corp.
52 Oakland Ave. N.
E. Hartford, CT 06108

203-522-2116
Multimate

Software Arts
27 Mica Lane
Wellesley, MA 02181
617-237-4000
VisiCalc, VisiFile

Software Publishing Corp.
1901 Landings Dr.
Mountain View, CA 94043
415-962-8910
PFS: Report, File, Graph

Stoneware, Inc.
50 Belvedere St.
San Rafael, CA 94901
415-454-6500
DB Master

Tandy Corp.
1800 One Tandy Center
Fort Worth, TX 76102
817-390-3700
Scripsit, Superscripsit

Glossary

Applications program: Software written in a high-level programming language that instructs the computer to perform a specific set of tasks.

Asynchronous: A mode of operation of a device or communications signal whereby the execution of the next instruction or event is initiated upon completion of the previous command or event.

Auto start: A common feature of many newer microcomputer systems, allowing the user to begin operation of the system simply by pressing a button.

BASIC: Beginner's All-purpose Symbolic Instruction Code, a high-level language originally developed at Dartmouth College. Extensions to this language have incorporated character string manipulation and improved input-output instructions.

Batch processing: A procedure in which a number of transactions to be processed by a computer are accumulated and processed together. The user has no access to the program during processing, as he would with online or interactive systems.

Binary digit: Commonly referred to as a bit (a contraction of "binary digit"), the smallest unit of information in the binary system used by computers. A bit is a representation of one or zero. It is the combination of bits that represents the data.

Bit: See **Binary digit.**

Board: A plastic component card that plugs into the bus of a microcomputer system. Individual boards typically handle individual functions, such as control of peripheral devices or processing. The bus of a microcomputer is often referred to as a "mother board" because of the slots it contains, so that boards controlling other functions may be plugged into it.

Bug: An error in a program.

Bus: The circuits used to conduct electronic signals or power to one or more units within a computer system. Different components of the bus connect registers, memory, peripheral devices and power supplies.

Byte: A group of adjacent binary digits, usually eight, which contains the coded representation of a character or symbol defined within the character set of the computer system.

Cassette tape memory: A package that provides audio or digital recording of binary signals for inexpensive mass storage by microcomputer systems.

Cathode ray tube (CRT): A computer terminal for data display with a television-like screen.

Central processing unit (CPU): The part of a computing system that controls the interpretation and execution of machine instructions, including the necessary arithmetic, logic and control circuits to execute such instructions. Microcomputers use microprocessor chips for the CPU.

COBOL: COmmon Business-Oriented Language, a high-level language that uses English-like expressions designed for manipulation and processing procedures in business applications.

CODASYL: The COnference on DAta SYstems Languages, originally sponsored by the U.S. Department of Defense and serving as an advisory group to the American National Standards Institute (ANSI).

Code: A system of symbols for use in representing machine instructions.

Compiler: That portion of the operating system that converts higher-level languages into machine language operation codes.

CP/M: A trade name of Digital Research, Inc. for an operating system used on many microcomputers.

CPU: See **Central processing unit.**

Database management system (DBMS): A special set of programs that manage the storage, access, updating and maintenance of a database. Data are organized so that they may be retrieved via access programs by a number of different means independent of the organizing program logic itself. Formal database management systems have been approved by CODASYL. Often, microcomputer file management systems are referred to as database management systems. However, true database management systems offer much greater access to a greater number of records than file management systems.

Debug: To find the errors in a program and to correct them.

Disk drive: The mechanism used for mass random access storage of data including both the storage medium (disks) and the machinery to spin it at a controlled speed.

Disk operating system (DOS): Used as a generic term by vendors to indicate an operating system capable of handling mass memory hard or floppy disk storage.

Disk storage: A mass storage medium incorporating one or more magnetic disks that may be grouped into units called disk packs or cartridges if the disk is hard, or thin flexible plastic cases for floppy diskettes.

Documentation: The written description of the purpose, structure and use of a computer program.

Download: To move data from a larger computer system or file to a smaller one.

Dumb terminal: A terminal that only displays the characters sent to it and transmits characters entered on it; it cannot store or process data.

Field: A set of characters treated as a unit and used to store a defined kind of data, such as title or call number. Usually a subset of a record.

File: An organized collection of data.

Floppy disk: A flexible mass storage medium made of oxide-coated mylar, offering low cost random access storage for small amounts of data.

FORTRAN: An acronym for FORmula TRANslator; a high-level language using algebraic notation and primarily designed for scientific and mathematical problems.

Hardware: The physical equipment and components in a computer system.

Index: A means of determining the location of data in a file.

Input/output control: A unit of hardware and associated programmed routines that service and manage the reading and writing of instructions and data to and from memory and peripheral devices.

Interface: The point of communication between devices, or between devices and users.

Loading: The process of inputting a program or data from a peripheral device to the memory of the computer. See also **Auto start**.

Local Area Network (LAN): The communications equipment and protocols necessary to connect terminals or computers within a building, a group of buildings or small geographical area for shared use of data or for communicating.

MARC record: MAchine Readable Cataloging record, a standard of bibliographic description in machine-readable form, designed by the Library of Congress for communication of data.

Megabyte (MB): One million bytes.

Menu: A list of options displayed on a terminal from which the user can select in order to perform a function.

Microcomputer: A computer that uses a microprocessor chip as its central processing unit. Generally distinguishable from a minicomputer by lower price, processing speed and capacity.

Minicomputer: A physically compact digital device that has a central processing unit, at least one input-output device and a primary storage capacity of at least 4000 characters.

Modem: Modulator/demodulator; a device that makes computer signals compatible with communications facilities.

Operating system: Software that controls the overall operations of a computer, handling routine data transfer operations among computer components and peripheral devices and composed of utility programs such as sorts, link editors, loaders and compilers.

PASCAL: A high-level language originally designed to teach programming as a systematic discipline and to do systems-level programming. This language is now in wider use and receiving attention as a desirable new system development language for library applications.

Peripheral device: A piece of equipment not part of the central processing unit, such as a disk storage device, magnetic tape reading unit, terminal or printer.

Precision: A term used to describe how accurately the records retrieved correspond to the search terms entered.

Privilege level controls: The ability to control the type of access each user has to the database and the type of operations allowed.

PROM: Programmable Read-Only Memory; nonvolatile memory capable of containing a specific program established by breaking circuit values within the chip.

Protocol: The standard or accepted format for transmission of data over a communications system.

RAM: Random Access Memory; a storage device in which the location of an individual address may be calculated, thus allowing random access. Also, RAM simply refers to general purpose main memory.

Random access: The ability to access data in a file directly without having to read the file sequentially to that point.

Read/write memory: Memory that can be both read from and written to, often used in referring to mass memory such as disk or tape.

Record: A group of data usually treated as a unit. A subset of ''file'' and a superset of ''field.''

ROM: Read-Only Memory; a storage device composed of circuits permanently programmed at the time of manufacture.

Software: The programs required in order for the computer to produce the desired results.

Synchronous: A mode of operation in which execution of instructions or events is controlled by a clock signal, usually at evenly spaced pulses.

System software: Operating system, compilers, assemblers and utilities.

Template: Software designed to be used in conjunction with other software.

Turnkey system: A complete system provided by a vendor, including hardware, software, installation and training.

Upload: To move data from a smaller computer, system or file to a larger one.

Video display terminal (VDT): See **Cathode ray tube.**

Suggested Reading List

AASL Committee for Standardization of Access to Library Media Resources. ''Microcomputer Software and Hardware—An Annotated Source List.'' *School Library Media Quarterly* (Winter 1984): 107.

Access: Microcomputers in Libraries. Oakridge, OR: DAC Publications (quarterly).

Advanced Technology/Libraries (AT/L). Published monthly by Knowledge Industry Publications Inc., 701 Westchester Ave., White Plains, NY 10604.

Archibald, Dale. ''What Is and What's to Come in Telecommunications, Part III.'' *Softalk* 3 (June 1983): 172.

Baker, Betsy, and Neilsen, Brian. ''Educating the Online Catalog User: Experiences and Plans at Northwestern University Library.'' *Research Strategies* 1 (Fall 1983): 155-166.

Chen, Ching-Chih, and Bressler, Stacey E., eds. *Microcomputers in Libraries.* New York: Neal-Schuman Publishers, Inc., 1982.

Computer Literacy Project. Report available from Tacoma Public Library, 1102 Tacoma Ave. S., Tacoma, WA 98402.

COSMIC: A Catalog of Selected Computer Programs. Published by the National Aeronautics and Space Administration. Available from the Computer Center Management and Information Center (COS-MIC), 112 Barrow Hall, University of Georgia, Athens, GA 30602.

Costa, Betty, and Costa, Marie. *Micro Handbook for Small Libraries and Media Centers.* Littleton, CO: Libraries Unlimited, 1983.

Datapro Reports. Several series: *Datapro 70: The EDP Buyers Bible; Minicomputers; Communications, Directory of Small Computers,* et al. Datapro Research Corporation, 1805 Underwood Blvd., Delran, NY 08075.

Desroches, Richard A. and Rudd, Marie. "Shelf Space Management: A Microcomputer Application." *Information Technology and Libraries* 2(2):187-189 (June 1983).

Dewey, Patrick R. *Public Access Microcomputers: A Handbook for Librarians.* White Plains, NY: Knowledge Industry Publications, Inc., 1984.

D'Ignazio, Fred. *The Star Wars Question & Answer Book About Computers.* New York: Random House, 1983.

Duncan, Carol S. "Compulit: Computer Literacy for Tacoma." *Library Journal* (January 1984): 52-53.

Edmonds, Leslie. "Taming Technology: Planning for Patron Use of Microcomputers in the Public Library." *Top of the News* 39 (Spring 1983): 247.

Epstein, Hank. "MITINET/retro: Retrospective Conversion on an Apple." *Information Technology and Libraries* 2(2):166-173 (June 1983).

Fosdick, Howard. *Structured PL/I Programming: For Textual and Library Processing.* Littleton, CO: Libraries Unlimited, 1982.

Freund, Alfred L. "Microcomputers: 'A New Era at Ramapo Catskill'." *Library Journal* 108(12):1217-1219 (June 15, 1983).

Genaway, David C. *Integrated Online Library Systems: Principles, Planning and Implementation*, White Plains, NY: Knowledge Industry Publications, Inc., 1984.

Glossbrenner, Alred. *The Complete Handbook of Personal Computer Communications*. New York: St. Martin's Press, 1983.

Henderson, Thomas B.; Cobb, Douglass Ford; and Cobb, Gena Berg. *Spreadsheet Software From VisiCalc to 1-2-3*. Indianapolis, IN: Que Corp., 1983.

Isshiki, Koichiro R. *Small Business Computers: A Guide to Evaluation and Selection*. Englewood Cliffs, NJ: Prentice-Hall, Inc., 1982.

Julien, Don and Schauer, Bruce. "Microcomputers Come to Kings County." *Library Journal* 108(12):1214-1216 (June 15, 1983).

Library Hi Tech (Published quarterly) and *Library Hi Tech News* (published eleven times per year). Published by Pierian Press, P.O. Box 1808, Ann Arbor, MI 48106.

Library Systems Evaluation Guides. 8 volumes. James E. Rush Associates, Inc., 2223 Carriage Rd., Powell, OH 43065-9703.

Library Systems Newsletter. Published monthly by Library Technology Reports, American Library Association, 50 E. Huron St., Chicago, IL 60611.

Library Technology Reports. Published bimonthly by the American Library Association, 50 E. Huron St., Chicago, IL 60611.

Loop, Liza. "Upper Arlington Computer Town Report." *Computer Town News Bulletin* 4 (May/June 1983): 1.

Mason, Robert M. "Searching for Software: Finding and Buying the 'Right Stuff'." *Library Journal* 107 (April 15, 1983): 801.

———."Traveling, Apple's LISA, Public Micros." *Library Journal* 108(12):1235-1236 (June 15, 1983).

Matthews, Joseph R. "Competition & Change: The 1983 Automated Library System Marketplace." *Library Journal* 109 (May 1, 1984): 853-860.

——— *Public Access to Online Catalogs: A Planning Guide for Managers.* Weston, CT: Online, Inc., 1982.

———; Lawrence, Gary S.; and Ferguson, Douglas K. *Using Online Catalogs: A Nationwide Survey.* New York: Neal-Schuman Publishers, Inc. 1983.

McWilliams, Peter. *The Word Processing Book.* Los Angeles, CA: Prelude Press, 1982.

Microcomputers for Information Management: An International Journal for Library and Information Services. Published quarterly by Ablex Publishing Corp., 355 Chestnut St., Norwood, NJ 07648.

Microcomputers for Libraries. Published quarterly by James E. Rush Associates, Inc., 2223 Carriage Rd., Powell, OH 43065-9703.

Online Libraries and Microcomputers. Published monthly by Information Intelligence, P.O. Box 31098, Phoenix, AZ 85046.

Online: the Magazine of Information Systems. Published six times a year by Online, Inc., 11 Tannery Lane, Weston, CT 06883.

Ouverson, Marlin. *Computer Anatomy for Beginners.* Reston, VA: Reston Publishing, 1982.

Roman, David R. "Word Processing: It's Never Been Easier." *Computer Decisions* 15(6):152-182 (June 1983).

Rosenberg, Victor. "The Personal Bibliographic System: A System for Creating and Maintaining Bibliographies." *Information Technology and Libraries* 2(2):184-187 (June 1983).

Sager, Donald J. *Public Library Administrators' Planning Guide to Automation.* Dublin, OH: OCLC, 1983.

Small Computers in Libraries. Published monthly (except July and August) by SCIL, Graduate Library School, College of Education, University of Arizona, 1515 E. First St., Tucson, AZ 85719.

"Special Section: ILS and LS/2000." *Information Technology & Libraries* 3 (June 1984): 144-173, 209-214.

Tolle, John E. *Public Access Terminals: Determining Quantity Requirements.* Dublin, OH: OCLC. 1984.

Verbesey, J. Robert. "Public Microcomputers on Long Island." *Library Journal* 108(12):1211-1213 (June 15, 1983).

Walton, Robert. *Microcomputers and the Library: A Planning Guide for Managers.* Austin, TX: Library Development Division, Texas State Library, 1982.

———. *Microcomputers: A Planning and Implementation Guide for Librarians and Information Professionals.* Phoenix, AZ: Oryx Press, 1983.

Wilburn, Gene and Wilburn, Marion. "Microcomputer-based Bulletin Board System: Free Videotext and Electronic Message Services." In *Microcomputers For Libraries: How Useful are They?*, edited by Jane Beaumont and Donald Kruger. Ottowa: Canadian Library Association, 1983.

Woods, Lawrence A., and Pope, Nolan F. *The Librarian's Guide to Microcomputer Technology and Applications.* White Plains, NY: Knowledge Industry Publications, Inc., 1983.

Index